Grant Us Your Peace

Grant Us Your Peace

Prayers from the Lectionary Psalms

David R. Grant

Chalice Press
St. Louis, Missouri

Biblical quotations, unless otherwise noted, are from the New Revised Standard Version Bible, copyright 1989, Division of Christian Education of the National Council of Churches of Christ in the USA. Used by permission.

Cover and interior design: Elizabeth Wright

This book is printed on acid-free, recycled paper.

Visit Chalice Press on the World Wide Web at
www.chalicepress.com

10 9 8 7 6 5 4 3 2 1   98 99 00 01 02 03

Library of Congress Cataloging–in–Publication Data

Grant, David R.
  Grant us your peace : prayers from the lectionary Psalms / by David R. Grant.
      p.   cm.
    ISBN 0-8272-1241-0
    1. Prayers.   2. Bible.   O.T.   Psalms–Meditations.   I. Title.
BV245.G63 1998
242 – dc21   98-34593
                                                                   CIP

Printed in the United States of America

For my Parents
Charles Jameson Croydon Grant
and
Gwladys Grant (née Jones)
who taught me most of my theology

Table of Contents

Foreword

David Grant brings to this fine manuscript the sensibilities and skills that are critical for pastoral ministry. Most important, those who practice pastoral ministry must know *what time it is*. And the clue is the calendar of the church year, so that "gospel time" is not according to shopping seasons or school semesters or sports schedules, but is according to the story we tell about the history of God known in Jesus. Grant knows about that time.

Second, pastoral ministry must know *what script counts when*, and so Grant relies upon the lectionary as a guideline for what we are to say when in the life and faith of the church. Most particularly, Grant pays attention to the psalms that are the deepest script of faithful utterance in the church. It is not without reason that there is currently a revived interest in the psalter in the church, to recover their use in "non-liturgical" churches and to use them more intentionally in more liturgical churches. The reason for this new interest, I have no doubt, is because women and men of faith (like other people) are being pushed by events to the "limit expressions" we need in order to embrace the limits of our experience we now face.

Third, pastoral ministry must know *what to do in times of extremity*. In a broad context of "trust and obey," more specifically what faithful people must do is pray, to speak the whole truth of life to the throne of God. David Grant is a person of prayer, able to lead a congregation as a people of prayer. And what these prayers consist in is uttering the script, the voice of our ancestors in faith, in our own voice, engaging in their cadences of faith in order to give effective cadence to our own sighs and groans.

In these prayers, Grant brings *time, script, and practice* together as an act of eloquence that does not call attention to itself, but is a willing vehicle for covenant, covenant embrace, and covenant dispute. These prayers, like every serious prayer, trust and assume that they are addressed to God, who hears. That is, this is not a psychological trick of auto-therapy, but it is real address, convinced of real hearing and real response.

The church is always again relearning, asking as the early disciples asked, "teach us to pray." David Grant does some teaching here, whereby we learn about *when* and *what* and *how* our "conversation of the heart" is conducted. Those of us who lead public prayer and those of us who pray secretly will be grateful to Grant for what he helps us say. For whether in public or in private, we do not pray *de novo*. We join the prayers that we have been praying back to our primal candor with God. Grant brings to this act of faith imagination, simplicity, devoutness — all those dimensions of faith that our world wants us not to practice.

Walter Brueggemann
Columbia Theological Seminary
March 2, 1998

Preface

In 1994, I was privileged to take study leave for one semester at Columbia Theological Seminary, Decatur, Georgia, U.S.A. I am grateful to Walter Brueggemann, Professor of Old Testament at Columbia, for providing me the particular insight into prayer as indicated in the introduction and for encouraging me to write.

I also thank the staff and students of Columbia Theological Seminary for one semester in their company, and the staff and students of Westminster College, Cambridge, England, for one term at their college in 1995.

My wife, Alison, typed the manuscript. My thanks and gratitude to her as typist, spell checker, grammarian, word processor, encourager, and protector of space. Thanks also to Jon L. Berquist for his encouragement.

David R. Grant
Knox Presbyterian Church
Dunedin, New Zealand
December 1997

Introduction

How do we match a prayer with the magnificent poetry of the Psalms? My guess is that we can't. But when we make the attempt, we may sow new seed and generate new fruitfulness. The motivation for writing these prayers is to open new doors for transformations, to use the Psalms' speech as our speech, and thus to entertain different configurations of our experience.

The prayers reflect on the Hebrew scriptures, specifically, the Jewish Psalms, which Christians have taken over, commandeered, and Christianized. For the most part I want to acknowledge their Jewishness, and so I seldom use the title "Christ." Christians will recognize the phraseology used, but I hope Jews might find the prayers useful as well. It is a significant reminder that Christians are not the only ones following the God of the Psalms.

The following reflections on Exodus 34:6–7 and Numbers 14: 18–19 form the basis of this modest volume. The thesis is that prayer can be understood as repeating back to God what God has already said to us.

Exodus 34:6–7 carries a phenomenal self-disclosure of God, which is given to, seen by, and more importantly, heard by Moses. Neither Moses, nor anyone so far in the present arrangement of the canon, has heard this combination of words before (but see Exodus 20:5–6). New, fresh words are spoken and heard on this new, fresh occasion — an occasion that comes in peculiar circumstances.

In the "golden calf" debacle (Exodus 32), Israel sought to slough off their leader and their liberating God, who was beyond their control. They sought a domesticated, obedient God who would act as they imagined any reasonable god ought to act — predictably, consistently, indulgently, satisfyingly. They did not count on the God of the ancestors acting powerfully against them.

Moses, at the very moment of Israel's revolt, was carrying in his hands the fresh covenant "written with the finger of God" (Exodus 31:18). An unsuspecting Moses got wind of their rebellion (Exodus 32:7ff.) through God's fierce wrath, which was vented on him. It took Moses by surprise; he pleaded for Israel's life in an eloquent and moving speech, and the narrator assures us that this speech changed God's mind (Exodus 32:11–14).

Moses, however, imitated God's anger, literally breaking the covenant (in effect broken already), and initiated violent retribution on

Israel (Exodus 32:25ff.). The narrator leaves us in no doubt as to who led Israel. Israel endured a plague (32:35) because of their making the calf, described with the terse note, "the one that Aaron made." At that point there were no other contenders for leadership, but Moses was still at a loss. How could he exercise leadership (Exodus 33:12ff.)? On the basis of favor in God's eyes (33:17), Moses was granted special and singular audience. With fresh cut stones over which he himself labored, he went up Mount Sinai into God's presence. Here he heard the Name, and the characteristics of the Name-bearer.

> The LORD descended in the cloud and stood with him there, and proclaimed the name, "The LORD." The LORD passed before him, and proclaimed,
> "The LORD, the LORD,
> a God merciful and gracious,
> slow to anger,
> and abounding in steadfast love and faithfulness,
> keeping steadfast love for the thousandth generation,
> forgiving iniquity and transgression and sin,
> yet by no means clearing the guilty,
> but visiting the iniquity of the parents
> upon the children
> and the children's children,
> to the third and the fourth generation."
>
> (Exodus 34:5–7)

Moses heard this magnificent, awe-inspiring, awe-full speech. The God, with reiterated Name (see 34:14), spoke from the mysterious mountaintop cloud — a proclamation uttered for Moses to hear.

The Name displayed God's inner life, God's intention, God's yearning and hopefulness for a chosen people. But the Name also preserved independence. This God would give all for the sake of the people, but this God would not be presumed upon. Always there was freedom to act in either of two ways (compare 34:6–7a and 34:7b). This covenantal relationship was and is, however, alive, current, always present.

Moses' response to the new speech was to worship; he was quite overcome by this eruption of generosity and favor but still had the wit to hear and repeat the new element not heard before — divine forgiveness in the face of human rebellion.

As the story unfolded, God was prepared to enter into a new covenant (Exodus 34:10ff.). How much of that depended on Moses' intercession? The question opened up new possibilities for engaging God. It is imperative that we today engage God in some form of conversation. But what language shall we employ to grab God's attention?

Numbers 14 contains another speech similar to the Exodus 34 revelation. Forty-six chapters of the canon had elapsed since Moses faced the Name and heard the proclamation. Israel had moved from Sinai to within reach of the land of promise. They survived on wilderness fare — enough for each, yet sparse enough to arouse pangs of nostalgia for a culinary fare distorted by distance and time (see Numbers 11:4–6); the "good old days" always dominate some people in times of transition.

Their "strong craving" (v. 4) consumed their attention to the exclusion of all else, and Moses bore the weight of complaint. God's immediate response was a scheme to bear the burden (v. 16ff.), and an emergency flight of alternative food (v. 31ff.). But God's response bore the marks of frustration to the point of bitter disappointment; the weight of the revelation of Exodus 34 was swinging toward the second half — "yet by no means clearing the guilty" (Exodus 34:7b).

The last straw came at the public hearing of the spies' report of the land of promise (Numbers 13). Crisis engulfed the whole enterprise, affecting every soul in the camp. Disillusionment, fear, frustration, passionate speeches of despair, hasty lobbying on the floor of the assembly to formulate alternative plans — all this frenzied activity followed the spies' speech.

A few clung desperately to the original resolution as outlined in Exodus 3:7–10. Moses and Aaron, the old hands, and Joshua and Caleb, the young hopefuls, engaged in the forlorn and impossible task of convincing all Israel that a rehashed past was bankrupt and that Pharaoh's relentless brick quota system offered no reward because it offered only death below the poverty line. The only future worth talking about was the one God had outlined — indeed offered — just across the river (Numbers 14:5–9)! But the people's hearts turned to stone (14:10), impervious to any plea, any hopeful future, and any word that remained true to the promise of God.

The crisis entered the heart of God, who was not immune to the people's fierce, resentful outburst. God formulated an alternative plan, too. It was simple, decisive, and uncomplicated. Destroy and begin again! Moses would be the new seed (14:12), so Moses was offered a future free of the discontent of the years.

In the moments Moses had to ponder the possibility, he forgot that he was slow of tongue (Exodus 4:10); he forgot his reliance on Aaron, his mouthpiece (4:16); and he forgot that he was on holy ground surrounded by the overpowering glory. Moses launched forth with desperate and remarkable eloquence.

Was it a rush of adrenaline in the fervor of the moment that enabled him to speak? Or was it the fear that the future of God's people rested on him and not on the forebears Abraham and Sarah that goaded him into speaking, that would be too great to bear? Or was it the sheer frustration of an unfinished project into which he had invested so much that provoked such speech? Who knows? And where did he get this speech?

He has practiced some of it before in a similar crisis (Exodus 32:11 ff.). In Numbers 14:15, he appealed to God's sense to avoid shame among the nations, particularly the oppressive Egyptians, who could kill and destroy just as ruthlessly as God proposed.

Moses interceded, dared to confront God, in a way reminiscent of Abraham at the site of Sodom (Genesis 18:25). But Moses went further in his intense attempt to avert crisis. Moses found new words, new speech, new language which, for him, generated new power, new courage to face up to the all-powerful Name. He recalled the speech of another occasion (Exodus 34:6–7), and he used that speech against God. He employed God's own speech so that God was now the listener and he, the intercessor, was the speaker. Moses reminded God of the speech spoken from the cloud.

> And now therefore, let the power of the Lord be great in the
> way that you promised when you spoke, saying,
>   "The Lord is slow to anger,
>   and abounding in steadfast love,
>   forgiving iniquity and transgression,
>   but by no means clearing the guilty,
>   visiting the iniquity of the parents
>   upon the children
>   to the third and fourth generation."
> (Numbers 14:17–18)

Moses refreshed God's memory of the words that emerged from God's own mouth at the moment of re-covenanting in Exodus 34:6–7. Moses did not repeat all God had said, but the words of Moses' prayer carried in essence the speech of re-covenanting.

Moses suggested that real power is to have the *ability* to execute death, but to refrain from doing so, on the basis of the surging powers — slowness of anger, steadfast love, and capacity to forgive — that make up the heart of God.

The Name listened and pondered, in the space between verses 19 and 20 (of Numbers 14), then made judgment: "I do forgive" (v. 20)! The crisis is averted, although not without consequences. Those who had seen God's glory, yet had tested God "these ten times," would not see the land promised to the ancestors. Only the faithful and the descendants would possess it. The tension is relaxed, and the profound dilemma is resolved, at least in part. There is always the temptation in narrative and in life to engineer complete resolution, to banish all ambiguity and uncertainty. Was that temptation in the heart of God with the suggestion of a new start with Moses and his seed?

As the story unfolds, the tension is relaxed but sufficiently maintained to admit an event-full, propelling future. The ambiguity will not go away, and the relationship will not slide into either a stagnant apathy of no expectation and no commitment or into the fulfillment of sufficiency and complete accord. For the time being, at Numbers 14:20–25, the future, which moments ago was threatened with complete collapse, now has a new, fresh chance.

I propose that is how all futures (as opposed to repeated pasts) have a chance. They are generated by the fresh articulating of the words already spoken. Prayers are a reflection of words already given; prayers in our mouths, where we are the speakers in the presence of the originator of the word, spawn new action in old circumstance both for God and for the pray-er.

So, what language shall we employ to grab God's attention? We repeat back to God what God has already said to us. The very speaking of God's old words into fresh constructions yields new frameworks, attitudes, and receptiveness, and generates new opportunity for God and for humanity.

Hence these psalms, held by the religious community to contain the word of God, are a source of generating power when we hold them up as prayerful mirrors to the Name from whence they came.

A Note on Usage

My practice is to use the lectionary psalm for Sunday to inform the theme for worship. The psalm and prayer following open a variety of doors into God's and our experience of life. Over a period of three years, the Psalms offer broad possibility for those who engage the biblical text — possibility for both God and us to revisit our own stories through the lens of the ancient stories.

I seek cohesiveness between text and prayer, and the prayers in this book are my attempt to articulate that coherence. The prayer is not a paraphrase; it uses the psalm as a springboard for speech. Often, although not always, the prayer takes on the form indicated in the reflection on Exodus 34 and Numbers 14 — to repeat back to God what God has already said. Further, as a parish minister who seeks to make worship liturgically cohesive, I needed an idea from within the liturgy to work on for the prayer theme. The psalm provided it, and what follows is my contribution to the liturgies of all ministers and leaders who use this book. The prayers may also prove useful in private devotion.

In worship, I read the prayer after the reading of the psalm; that's where the prayer is seeded. The prayers are crafted for public liturgy, where the off-balancing rawness of psalm and prayer are held by the safe order of public liturgy, much the same as the harrowing exodus tradition is held in the psalms, before a backdrop of trusted creation orderliness.

Recently, I have begun to attach an assurance of pardon to the prayer, picking up the prayer's phrases and reiterating them in terms of our need for forgiveness, for example, "Now, Lord God, who will notice when we.... Jesus Christ may notice; but Jesus came not to condemn, but to forgive. I tell you in the name of Jesus Christ, you are forgiven." The response is "Thanks be to God."

Change the words as you see best; it is the people's best worship we seek to enhance, not adherence to someone else's form. May God grant you peace, shalom, in your public liturgy, your private preparing, and your private devotion.

Year A

THE YEAR
OF MATTHEW

PSALM 122

Someone addressed us;
    someone spoke to us and said,
"Let us go to the house of the Lord!"

Was it you, God of Israel, who invited us?
Was it you who called us to your home?
Was it you who wrote us into Sabbath liturgy,
    here within these walls,
        where many hundreds have come before,
        responding to your call?

We come in fearfulness for being found out:
    you know us too well.
We come in confidence, for we are baptized:
    you have called us before.
We come in prayer for all your people:
    your peace is our desire.

The reputation of our forebears in the faith
    is at stake,
        so we must live a life of peace.

The reputation of your home, this place of worship,
    is at stake,
        so we must convey the life of peace.

Your own reputation is at stake, Lord our God,
    so we must seek the goodly life of peace for all.

May peace settle in our anxious, troubled, fretful hearts,
    at least for this hour.

We pray in the name of the trouble-breaker,
    peace-maker,

AMEN.

PSALM 72:1–7, 18–19

Your people Israel sought a king who would enact
    your mode of justice,
    your mark of righteousness
    among people of poverty.
In this place, we children of your people
    dare to seek a Lord who would
    enact in us your style of justice,
    your kind of righteousness.

May the earth bring forth its goodness for all
    and the land produce fruit enough
    that not one may starve.

May those who harvest the earth's fruit,
    and those who sell, buy, and distribute it,
    do so with maximum justice and minimum greed.

May our sought-for Lord
    defend the dispossessed,
    deliver the hopeless,
    and break the power of deathly manipulators of power.

May our sought-for Lord live beyond
    the sun and moon running their courses.
May the Lord sweeten the soul of humanity,
    as rain sweetens the newly ploughed paddock.
May the Lord's days flourish abundantly.

We, the children of the children of Israel,
    bless you, O God.
In this room of your many-roomed mansion
    where your glory is honored,
    we bring glory to your name,

AMEN.

PSALM 146:5–10

God of Jacob,
>maker of heaven and earth
>keeping faith with all you have made,

We will say these words of the Psalm
>but we may not believe them,
>whether you keep faith or not.

No wonder our lives are strewn with ruin,
>and our wicked way is all that's known and acted on.

No wonder.

God of Jacob,
I am the prisoner of distorted imagination,
>of little dream,
>of minute hope and no wonder.

I need to hear fresh words, like
>execute justice
>give food
>set free
>open eyes
>lift up
>love
>watch over
>uphold.

Then, God of Jacob, when these words become my text,
>you will reign,
>and our fresh, free imagination, dream, hope, and wonder
>may enliven our living
>and determine our well-being.

In the name of one who freely imagined new life for all,

AMEN.

PSALM 80:1–7, 17–19

We come, just days before Christmas,
    tired, exhausted, anxious, depleted.
Have we bought enough?
Have we bought too little?
Have we bought the right gift?
Have we forgotten to buy for someone?

Has someone forgotten us?!

Give ear to our anxieties, we pray,
    you who lead us.

Lead us out of our frayed nervousness
    into your courtly, regal presence.
Stir yourself! Come and save us!
Restore us! Shine your face on us!
Then we may be saved!

Through the year, we have had our season of weeping,
Tears have come in our moments of abandonment,
Frustration is compounded by your distance from us
    and secular society's taunt of irrelevance.

Restore, Lord God; restore, restore, restore,
    as we ready ourselves to hold your promised child.

In the name of the one who gives
    and brings forth light,

AMEN.

PSALM 96

A psalm which calls us to praise the God who comes in judgment?
Lord, these two ideas don't fit together.

Yes, we will praise you,
    and we will recognize how the whole of creation bursts forth
    in praise of its maker.
With all the church families of the world
    we join to acknowledge who you are,
    we bring the offering of ourselves,
    and we come into your place.

But can you be serious that you judge us?
We have done so well to get here
    and we don't take kindly
    to coming voluntarily to the place of judgment.

Unless — unless your judgments on us
    are different from the condemnation we expect of judges.
Could you judge us
    and fondly hold us at the same time?
Could you welcome our shortcomings
    as springboards for life? And better life?
Could you place truth before us
    that will entice us to move, to grow?

As you look on us,
    would you see Christ our brother standing with us,
    pleading our cause?
Lord God, Judge and Savior,
    don't leave us as lonely orphans, battling by ourselves,
    forlornly seeking to fill our days
    so as to ward off boredom, or truth.
Heavenly Father, loving like the best of mothers,
    take our battered, hopeful lives to yourself,
    that we today may be loved,
    intensely loved.

In Jesus Christ's name,

AMEN.

PSALM 97

Today   — light dawns, Christ is born;
             — light is sown, Christ is known.

Today   — joy is given, God's new heaven;
             — earth's renewal, for God's faithful.

Today   — new words spoken, old ways broken;
             — rescue mounted, Christ exalted.

Today   — breakers breaking, praise in making;
             — mountains heaving, glory brightening.

Today   — creation bows, we worship now;
             — rejoicing glad, Christ our Lord.

Today   — gift exchange, but more is offered;
             — child in arm, savior, prophet.

AMEN.

PSALM 98

Lord God, newness abounds;
> the always-novel event of a newborn
> envelops us with joy;
> holy power has happened;
> victory of right over wrong reveals itself.

You remembered.

You remembered the house of Israel,
> and all those adopted into that home.
You have offered us a future,
> a future in the world,
> a future for the earth and its peoples.

So we respond with joy,
> a joy born of amazement and wonder,
> a joy-bearing song of praise.

Our highly strung temperaments generate
> a harmony beyond our capability.
Our usually tensioned bodies produce
> a unison concord of peace greater than ourselves.
Our normally blustery lives together compose
> a well-tuned body of people in praise of you.

With all creation we stand in awe,
> unable to contain ourselves for joy at your signature
> writ large
> in small type
> in this child.

In his name we pray,

AMEN.

PSALM 148

Every corner of creation praises you, O God:

— the heavens, and heaven's angels sing to the counterpoint
    of earth and earth's creatures
— the heavens and heavenly bodies dance to the quickstep
    of earth and earthly features.

You spoke and everything was joyfully created;
Now everything speaks, and you are brought to joyful presence
    in hearts and minds.

May we join creation's chorus
    these last days of the year,
so that our year past is redeemed by praise,
and the year to come is founded on praise.

Then in concert with all you have made,
the harmony reverberating through creation's praise,
may strike the chord of well-being among your people,
and our lives together resound in rich symphony.

For your glory, and our salvation,

AMEN.

PSALM 147:12–20

Lord God, we bring our minds to engage your mind,
      we bring our hearts to engage your heart,
      we bring our wills to engage your will.

We fight through our technologically loaded minds,
      our disinterested jaded hearts,
      our carefully rationalized wills,
      to hear again and afresh
            your standing in your world,
            your caress of creation,
            your passionate interest in your people.

Lord God, whom we seek to engage,
      embrace us with your words of blessing
      and clothe us with peace granted;
      amaze us with your attention to patterned weather
            — sometimes furious, sometimes gentle,
      and astound us with the blessedness of our babies,
            — sometimes gentle, sometimes furious.
May your swift word pierce our armor
      of technology, disinterest, and reason,
      that we may hear your bidding
      and live your gracious instruction,
      as we hear no one else.

In the name of the One free and obedient,

AMEN.

PSALM 72:1–7, 10–14

Who will bring justice to the earth?
Who will oversee fairness among the peoples?
Who will moderate equity between the nations?
> The one who bears God's justice.
> The one who carries God's sense of fairness.
> The one who conveys God's equity.
But who will see that justice is done?
Who will determine fairness?
Who will deliver equity?

It is the King —
> bearer of justice, counsel for fairness, adjudicator of equity.
The King will secure justice for the poor
> and fairness for the disadvantaged and equity for the needy.
Then there will be security and well-being
> and enlightenment and guarantee of liberty for all.

But who will make it happen in our world?
The King's daughter? The King's son?
The King's follower? The King's disciple?
Those who imitate the King?

O God, is that possible?
Because we are the satisfied who believe we are the needy;
> we are the rich who believe we are poor;
> we are the strong who believe we are weak;
> we are the oppressors who believe we are oppressed.

Our lives are ambiguous, mixed, complex,
> incongruent, double-triple-minded.
Are we still precious in your sight?
Lord God, teach us to practice justice, employ fairness, render equity
> within ourselves and for others;
being true to the King and servants to our world.

In the name of the servant King,

AMEN.

PSALM 29

The creative word of the Lord God again
      peals across the universe
      and resonates in our hearts.
The voice of the creator booms forth
      and echoes across the ages,
      through these walls,
      enough to make even stolid hearts quaver.

Lord God, we are reluctant to believe the world we live in
      is shaky and temporary.
They have led us to believe it was reliable and permanent,
      safe and certain.

But it crumbles, breaks up, and breaks down.
So we are anxious, and we work harder,
      and we worry more;
      and our time carries an urgency,
      putting us on edge,
      edging us toward the very chaos we seek to avoid.
May we freshly hear the ancient
      "Let there be…and it was good,"
and so exchange our pressured time
      for communion time,
      where once more we may freely and joyfully
      ascribe to the only strengthener,
      attribute to the only enthroned one
      the power to hold together.

In the name of the One first baptized,

AMEN.

PSALM 40:1–11

It's me, O Lord, standing in the need of prayer.
It's me, O Lord.
I cry to you, out of my pitiful self,
    bogged down in pettiness and petulance,
      longing to hear steadfast love and faithfulness in my ears.
It's me, O Lord, and I hear.

Somehow my ears command my feet;
    what I hear makes a new step possible.
Somehow my feet step out and up,
    and my mouth responds to my hearing;
    a new song, a song of praise.

It has occurred to me to increase my offering,
    to make payment for services rendered.
But no; I find you have a record of me in life's book.
    You have taken account of me,
    and you have multiplied in return what little I can give.
I am a small player
    and I cannot compete in the giving business.
So how can I respond?
You have touched my ears, my feet, my mouth.
Now touch my heart with gracious law
    and let me return to your people
    the words you have given;
    your glad news, your saving help,
    your deliverance, your faithfulness,
    your steadfast love.

We all stand in the need of prayer, O Lord.
Hear our cry
    and lift us all to newness of song and heart.

In the name of the One who could,

AMEN.

PSALM 27:1, 4–9

God, we would not say "Whom shall I fear?"
    if we were not afraid.
We would not say "Of whom shall I be afraid?"
    if we felt no threat.
We would not ask to be hidden in shelter
    if we perceived no gathering clouds of storm.
We would not request concealment under cover,
    if we sensed no exposure to searing danger.
We would not seek your lifting us up out of harm's way
    if we were unaware of the shifting sands under our feet.

In our more honest moments, our God, we acknowledge how risky life is,
    how perilously close we come to grief,
    how fragile is our human predicament,
    how our lives are in jeopardy day by day.

Sometimes we deny our tenuous grasp on life,
    going on our drugged, merry way;
and sometimes we succumb to life's terror,
    not venturing into life's risk.

But here, in your house, this day we defiantly sing,
    surrounded as we are by the forces of evil and death.
In the presence of our enemies we joyfully bring our praise.
So listen to us!
In this moment of truth,
    where we see our lives surrounded by menace,
    hear us!
If you don't, we are alone indeed.
If you do, we will face tomorrow,
    we will dare venturing into the coming week,
    under the gaze of your countenance,
    confident of your companionship.

In the name of the companion Christ,

AMEN.

PSALM 15

Lord, you can count us out of your dwelling place,
    and way beneath your holy mountain.

In a rare brush with honesty, we say:
    We often deserve blame.
    Wrong too readily renders our attempts at truth as a lie.
    We know too well how to slander, albeit ever so politely.
    Friend or neighbor has no ultimate protection
        against our fearful defensiveness.
    We court the wicked and snicker at the honorable.
    Our promises are easily broken; we make a living out of interest.
    The innocent suffer under our urgent lobbying.

We are easily moved,
    we quickly change our allegiance, we act defiantly.
Yet here we are,
    with confession on our lips and shame in our hearts,
    seeking an abiding place,
    dwelling for the moment within earshot of your holiness,
    willing to hear a teaching to save us.

Stabilize our lives for the moment:
    that we may make our acquaintance
    with blamelessness and rightness,
    befriend heartfelt truth,
    renounce slander and evil,
    and firmly embrace neighbor and friend.

Set our foot steady for the moment, that we may
    repudiate wickedness and cultivate a fear of the holy other,
    participate in promise-making and promise-keeping,
    entertain interest-free lending and rewarding life
        without ulterior motives.
So may we, for this hour, occupy the stable place of your presence,
    Holy One of Israel,
    that we may view our shifting lives
    and make the adjustments we can.

In the name of the abiding One,

AMEN.

PSALM 112

We know, Lord God, what it is to be wicked.
Our diffuse desires came to nothing;
  our anger at anything and everything in general
    withered our souls;
  our teeth ground in frustration
    at our incoherent, frenzied, distraught lives.

We were bound and further bound when reminded of the bind,
  with no way out to unbounded joy;
  and the lie of controlled joy only made the binding
    more secure and harder to break.

May our praise this day be the gateway to freedom,
  and our nervousness at being in your holy presence
  release the energy to sing our souls silly for joy.

We seek to live within your commands.
We seek to pass on the blessings you gave us to a generation to come.
We seek to give as you have given us.

May the light of your presence we carry
  be a light to all our acquaintances.
May the justice of our dealings bring justice to the community.
May the resilience you cultivate in us withstand the shattering of evil.
Though we become afraid, fear will not rule us.
Though enemies surround us,
  we will follow the agenda of the victorious One.
Though riches are showered on us,
  we will be in a giving, not hoarding, frame of mind.

In the name of the righteous One,
  who lived the life we would hunger for,

AMEN.

PSALM 119:1–8

Lord, our God, we are learners in your school;
      we are practicing people of faith;
      we are yet to become competent, knowing, wise,
          conversant in your academy, excellent in ethics.
But we are more than beginners,
      beyond playschool.
We know enough to fear forsakenness and to fly from shame,
      because forsakenness and shame, even when chosen and
          self-inflicted,
      debilitate us and render us helpless.

So we cry to you — that our attendance here may be steadfast,
      our eyes focused on your code of practice,
      and our hearts urgently seeking your marching orders
          for our walk with you.

Then we are bold to praise you
      for the hour; forgiven and innocent,
      unstained, with noble intent;
      complete, replete enough
      until our return to school
      next week.

In the name of the One who called disciples to himself,

AMEN.

PSALM 119:33–40

Lord, our God, Christians and Jews for centuries have called you
    "Our God."
They have prayed to you,
    pleaded with you, praised you, thanked you,
    cursed you, struggled with you, become angry with you.
They have sought your blessing,
    brought their children to you,
    asked for forgiveness from you,
    covenanted together before you in marriage,
    committed their dying to you.
They have found you to be their comforter in their distress,
    their teacher in their ignorance,
    their goad in their apathy,
    their solid rock in their insecurities,
    their friend to whom they can return.
God, we demand much of you.

At our whim and fancy,
    we ignore you, come to you when it suits,
    blame you, use your name as a curse,
    call to you when we are at our wits' end,
    give to you, *if* we have anything left over,
    take our enjoyment from your creation.
And yet you come,
    with invitation again,
    with graciousness again;
and here, in the psalm, with command and law,
to lead us into harmony, peace, unity, trust, and our own wholeness.

So here, we make the choices:
between ignoring you, subservience to you, or companionship with you;
between no obedience, blind obedience, or faithful obedience;
between flouting laws, rule by laws, or guidance by your words to us.

So Lord our God,
    as the saints of old have struggled with being faithful
        in a less than best world,
    be with us in our struggle of faithfulness.

In the name of the Messiah, the faithful One,

AMEN.

PSALM 131

Mother of Israel and mother God,
　　you gently lead us, and feed us.

We do not need the fighting arrogance
　　that struggles with life, and time, and neighbor.

We question the value of ambition
　　that must desperately grasp initiative for survival.

We wonder at the wisdom of self-assertion
　　that blinds us to everyone but me.

For you are our hope, freeing us from imprisoned life,
　　and imagined meager time, and perceived threatening neighbor.
You are our future, freeing us from rigid, calculated planning.

You clothe our new self,
　　freeing us from a fearfully fine focus on me alone.
Our child within rejoices, skips for joy,
　　　enjoined by a God so tender,
　　　so thoughtful, so generous with satisfaction,
　　　offering us a future of careful abandonment and secure
　　　　joyfulness.

Thanks be to God.

In the name of the Son of Mary,

AMEN.

PSALM 2

Lord, God of nations,
With dismay and helplessness we watch the conniving powerful
  carve out with renewed greed another land,
  another company, another publicly-owned utility.

They seem to have no sense of responsibility,
  no willingness to serve,
  no regard for consequences for others.
Most of us seem inconsequential nonentities,
  insignificant, expendable, of negligible importance.

But we know of you: a God of laughter,
  a God of loud, hearty laughter,
  chuckling, chortling, giggling, twinkling,
  hooting, pealing, gales of laughter;
  laughter of derision and ridicule
  at perishing attempts at power wielding.

Don't they know? Haven't they heard?
Has no one told them who it is who builds up, and breaks in pieces?
We will tell — today we tell.
  Because we are begotten in the family — called daughters, sons;
  so we have heard that to belong is to serve,
  and companionship is worship,
  and to keep company with you
   is to live and breathe, saved from perishing,
  a refuge, protected by laughter, kindled by love.

Blessed are we.
Praise be to you, O God.

AMEN.

PSALM 32

Lord our God,
> we would not wish to be described as stupid as an ass
> or as dopey as a donkey,
>> who must be coerced into acting properly.
Yet Lord God, when your ways are set out clearly before us,
> and we choose not to take notice,
> maybe we deserve mule status.

You sound like a God eager to teach,
> eager to counsel, eager to preserve in times of trouble,
> and while we resolutely ignore you,
> you persistently come to us.

We confess to you the silence of our hearts:
> the secrets that we have hidden out of shame,
> the deceit we have lived by —
>> they waste away our spirits and bodies.

Yet you, and only you, can deal with our secrets.
Only you can lift shame from our spirits.

Lord God, we acknowledge the secrets, the hidden sin of our hearts.
And we pray for forgiveness.

So now, give us the courage to enter into happiness.
> May a blessed future be ours because sin is covered.
> May enjoyment of your creation be ours
>> because we no longer have to hide.
> May we be a free people,
>> in conversation with you and with each other,
>> able to love and be loved,
>> and to trust and be trusted.

In the name of the One you entrusted to us,

AMEN.

PSALM 121

One I look to the mountains; where will my help come from?

Many We look to mountains, seas, land, institutions,
and we know that ultimate help doesn't come from there.

One My help will come from the Lord, who made heaven and
earth.

Many Our greatest hopes and biggest dreams
find their life around you, Lord of heaven and earth.

One He will not let you fall; your protector is always awake.

Many God, some of us are falling; some of us feel unprotected,
and sometimes it seems as though you are asleep.

One The protector of Israel never dozes or sleeps.

Many But perhaps you leave us to experience wilderness.
Perhaps when left alone we discover the important.

One The Lord will guard you; he is by your side to protect you.

Many Continue to guard us, Lord; continue to be at our side even if
we feel alone.

One The sun will not hurt you during the day, nor the moon
during the night.

Many So, protector God, keep us from burnout through too much
doing, trying to solve problems through busyness and
excessive moonlighting.

One He will protect you as you come and go, now and forever.

Many So, Lord, in our coming and going through your world,
give us the confidence of hope-filled people, now and forever.

AMEN.

PSALM 95

We come, O God, to sing, to worship with joyful noise.

Even though we may feel floored by the week,
    flattened by our circumstance,
so that our talk is in monotone
and our souls are in monochrome
and our eyes have lost their dancing.

Yet we are here in your presence;
    here to accept the gift of time,
      and the gift of opportunity to be secured again to You,
        the rock of our salvation.

Great God, above all the other lesser gods we may name,
    the very ground we walk on is yours,
    the very air we breath in is yours,
    all that makes our environment a delight is yours.

So we come — worshiping, kneeling before you,
    our Lord and Maker —
    as people ushered into a safe place.

May it be today that we hear you;
    soften our wills, our hardness, our masks, our impenetrable selves;
so that your anger, your disgust,
    is diverted away from our rigid but fragile selves.

And may we find the way into your rest.

In the name of the One who brings peace,

AMEN.

PSALM 23

Lord God, our lives are touched by a rich array of experiences:
　　　　some we would wish for, some we would not wish;

　　　led by a caring shepherd-like One,
　　　given days of rest so that our souls are restored;

　　　valleys of darkness — even the deep darkness of death,
　　　promise of companionship;

　　　feast tables in spite of enemies,
　　　overflowing cups,
　　　a holy presence over our lives.

Lord, our God, we are people who need to hear you:
　　　some of us need your close care right now;
　　　some of us need days of rest and restored souls —
　　　　　may we find you in our busyness;
　　　some of us know the dark shadows of life right now;
　　　and some of us know the dark shadows of death;
　　　　　bring light and life to our despairing dismay,
　　　　　so that we are not alone.
　　Some of us feel surrounded by enemies —
　　　　　people, powers, or systems
　　　　　that are relentless and unbending —
　　　　　may we find food for our souls,
　　　　　and a feasting challenging the power of oppression;
　　　some of us are grateful to overflowing,
　　　　　and our gratitude comes to you today as an offering;
　　　some of us are simply happy to be in your presence,
　　　　　a people held our whole life long.

Hear our prayers.

In the name of the One who leads as a shepherd,

AMEN.

PSALM 130

We watch;
      we wait.

Desolate souls, yearning, craving, thirsting,
      for homecoming and parental love.

Mostly we can ignore our orphan status,
      claiming ancestry, pedigree, forebears.

A good part of our time is spent in diverting pursuits,
      cherishing competencies, or failure, or both.

More often than not, we will not face our loneliness,
      finding escape with friends or acquaintances.

But here, in worship, in quiet prayer,
      souls exposed to grace unbounded,
      we cannot hide.
Nor do we want to hide.

Out of the depths we cry! Hear us, O Lord!
You said you would forgive.
Forgive us now, each one,
      and clear the way to our God-given home.

Redeem, restore, repair,
      that we may know your steadfast love.

In the name of the Redeemer we pray,

AMEN.

PSALM 118:1–2, 19–29

Lord God, creator, founder, builder;
the One who has an eye for sound building material;
the One who discerns a faultless cornerstone,
    where most see rejects;
God, you are our hope.

Lord God, maker of days, crafter of lives,
    may we enter into your righteous presence
    with attire redesigned by righteousness.

As you cast your perceptive eye on us,
    see us as people clothed in Christ-like righteousness,
    worthy of the festal procession.

For you, O God, you are our hope.

And now may our inner lives reflect our outer garb;
    for we are a people whose inner lives require attention.
If others knew what we know,
    we would be banned from the march.
If we dared to admit to our dubious secrets,
    we would be railed out of court.
If, in our honesty, we were to make judgment on ourselves,
    we would slink away ashamedly.

So attend to us, for you, O God, are our hope.

Attend to us with the same attention you give chief cornerstones,
    but with saving eye,
    redeeming intent,
    and blessedness that lifts us heavenward.

For you, O God, you are our hope.

In the name of the Chief Architect's Assistant,

AMEN.

PSALM 31:9–16

Lord God, amidst the celebration of today,
    we know the gathering shadows,
    the impending deadness,
    which weighs heavy.

Keep trust in you alive, we earnestly pray,
    as the world goes on its ponderous, sometimes cruel, way.

Keep us faithful to you, we ask,
    as the gravity of life descends.

Keep our confidence in you vital,
    as the darkness of this week envelops us.

May our weeping and desolate pain turn us toward you
    and away from bitterness.

May our crying and tears restore us to your presence
    and away from separation.

May our sorrows and tiredness make us yield to your strength
    and away from despair.

Turn us to yourself, Lord God,
    so that we may experience your kindness and constant love.

Then, whatever happens to us
    will be of no consequence.
    Our times are in your hands,
    our knowing is that you are dependable
    and will rescue us.

In the name of Jesus the Crucified,

AMEN.

PSALM 22

Lord God,
      the climax of your creative career was
      the blessed human creature.
What a glorious Friday — it was very good.

And the climax of your son's career,
      your most blessed human being,
      was utter, utter forsakenness.
What a dreadful Friday — it was accursed.

Have you ever liked a Friday since?
This Friday, called "Good," is the worst Friday of your life.
Forsaken Friday, complete abandonment Friday.
God — deaf on this Friday,
      hearing no cry in the day and no desperate call at night.
Only mockers watch —
      sarcastic, pious cynics, so certain of who will be saved;
only mockers take notice on this Friday,
but you of all gods, Lord of all our days,
you abandon a faithful one.

And we trusted you, as our ancestors trusted you,
      seeking shameless, trust-filled days.
But this shameful Friday,
      you turned and denied your blessed one.

God, Friday strains your credibility and strains our already shaky faith.

We retreat, too, for we are mystified, bewildered, even misled.
For Fridays were once glorious — but now utter disaster.

Save him, O God, and save us.

In the name of the Crucified,

AMEN.

PSALM 118:1-2, 14-24

Lord God,
       three days of hell
       and now you startle us with a newness beyond imagining.

Resurrection stretches our credibility;
       but there it is, claimed by the witnesses, stated in the word,
       sung by congregations the world over,
       with glad songs of victory.

Your power and resolve has done it, Lord God;
       your saving strength is shouted by every faithful community.

Because you let your beloved entombed one out,
       we now clamor to get in through the gates
       to where the news is announced
       and unprecedented thanks expressed.

For perishing is not now our destiny,
       and abundant living is more our natural habitat
       because the one who looked like a reject
       now holds us firmly in the place of glad celebration.

And it is all your doing, Lord, our God!

Gather us up in the glad procession of resurrection life, we pray.
Because last Friday was bankrupt,
       and that bitter taste is enough
       to convince us of where our hope lies.

This is the day you have made.
May this day flavor every day
       to our life's end.

AMEN.

PSALM 16

God, we can recount times of pleasure,
      story lines of good experience,
      boundary lines that have kept
           the unpleasant out and the pleasant in.

And so we bless you.

But we know we gather blind spots,
      and perpetuate injustice,
      and allow evil to roll on,
      gathering us inadvertently in its progress to hell.

So warn, counsel, instruct us,
      for our certainty mechanism falters,
      our vision clouds,
      and other gods wink seductively
           when we entertain their names.

You are the one, Lord God, who fills the seeker's cup.
You are the one who lays the lines of life.
You are the one who holds our inheritance.

And as we worship with our newly resurrected brother Christ,
      fresh from the tomb of death,
      lead us in life's paths,
      attend to our impaired vision,
      keep us in full presence with you,
      the one God, source of all goodness.

In the name of the Risen One,

AMEN.

PSALM 116:1–4, 12–19

God of speech, and God with listening ear,
    your word to us is clear.

As long as we remain uncommunicative, silent, speechless,
    we suffer in petrified distress with no hope.

But when our anguish moves us to cry out,
    we discover the way of salvation.

Lord God, that is not new to you, or your people.
We stand in the exodus tradition;
    people with the gumption, the courage,
    to cry out, to say what is in mind,
    and then to experience undreamed-of liberation.

How can we express salvation-motivated gratitude?
In the assembly of your people we say it;
    in the presence of your faithful family
        our dedicatory vows are repeated;
    with the other covenanted ones
        we reiterate our reflections of covenant;
that the dying and rising of your Chosen One
    provokes in us gratitude and hope;
that the oppressive policies of political power
    will not have the last say;
that even destructive personal motivations
    have mere temporary power.

But, Lord God, our truth-discovery and truth-bearing is alive
    only as long as we keep in conversation with you.

So hear our prayer, in the name of Word made flesh,

AMEN.

PSALM 23

Lord God, the one who gathers us at table,
  real tables, with bread-wine, food;
  here we gather at the table
    where sacrifice is regularly offered
    in restorative nourishment,
  where empty cups are brim-filled,
    and empty souls are refreshed;
  where imagined threat is melted,
    and real threat is rendered powerless.

We gather in your house, shepherd God,
  shepherded here by compelling love,
the place to be,
where new maps are drawn,
  new configurations of our world are formed,
  new structures for life are framed.

But we are not here to soak in static pools of peaceful boredom
  because the enemy is always at the door,
  lurking in dark shadow,
  seducing with mirage light.
And we know wiles of the enemy
  because sometimes the enemy is so like us.

Yet in this place
  we are free to rejoice in the presence of enemies,
  the table is again prepared and offered,
  and we are satisfied with good things.

Thanks be to God!

AMEN.

PSALM 31:1–5, 15–16

We admit to you, Lord God,
>what we hesitate to admit to each other:
>that we cannot manage our own lives.
We try to cover all bases,
>we allow for every contingency,
>we screen out every surprise that may threaten.
Yet still we are chased by some lurking shame,
>we are caught in web-net unanticipated,
>we are thrown by tangential probes unforeseen.

We cannot get our hands on the full processes of history;
We are players in a drama of authorship out of reach.

So, Lord God, righteous deliverer, creator of refuge,
>we turn to you in our dithered confusion,
>we appeal to you in our confession of uncontrolledness,
>we cry out to you our acquiescence in a drama tainted by anarchy.

And we hang on these words,
>"Into your hand I commit my spirit."

It is you, O God, who bends the ear to hear,
>it is you who redeems your people,
>it is your face which shines before us.

Our times are in your hand.
So save us, we pray, for your name's sake;
>even for your own reputation, rescue us.

AMEN.

PSALM 66:8–20

Lord, our God, a brief reflection on our national life
      reveals times of burden too great to bear,
      times of test, searing our public consciousness,
      times of communal dousing that submerge our perceptions,
      often trying us all to the edge of our endurance.

Yet we are still here.
We could argue the world was beyond your control.
We could conclude that you reject us.
We could believe you punish us.

But, no, we are still here, in this sanctuary
      bringing praise and offering
      for our living and not dying,
      for our place of space, with no threat of oppression.

From this communal space you grant each one a hearing.

So we come, to make our confessions
      and receive your forgiveness.

We are wise to our technique of cherishing sin,
      or at best mumbling inaudibly our confession prayers,
      which keeps us in limping control, ensuring non-forgiveness.

So we risk speaking, and risk your hearing,
      and risk a forgiveness-primed transformation,
      wrapped in steadfast love,
      signposting subversive testimony to all listeners
      that you, God, are above all gods;
      there is no other, and only you deserve our allegiance.

Thanks be to God.

AMEN.

PSALM 68:1–10, 32–35

Lord God, your book is full of stories of people saved from enemies,
    brutal enemies who melted before you,
      savage enemies who were dissipated like smoke in the wind.

Your book is full of stories of once-orphaned people, now come home,
    of widowed people now protected, of imprisoned people set free.

Your book is full of stories of thirsty people thirst-quenched,
    of hungry people satisfied,
    of disinherited people possessing restored heritage.

Even creation joined,
    rejoicing in awe-filled joy at deeds too wild to be imagined.

Lord God, we are in the same but different world.
We see cruelty beyond credence, brutality beyond belief,
    savagery beyond our worst conception.

We know of the displaced homeless, even those who live in a house;
we know of the unprotected at the mercy of merciless scavengers;
we know of imprisoned ones behind bars of ignorance,
    bars of alcohol, bars of twisted relationship.

We know of people thirsting in parched ideologies;
    people hungry for emotional, spiritual,
      intellectual, physical satisfaction;
    people lost in the present, lost in a historical vacuum.

How can your book help them? What testimony will set them free?
What witness will attest to any kind of fruitful future?

In this sanctuary, God of Israel,
    we reread and reiterate your book's claims,
    we give testimony to your powerful empowering,
    we witness to your heaven-sent command, directed earthward
      and embodied in this praise-singing body
      of your saved ones.

In the name of the Rising One in our midst,

AMEN.

PSALM 104:24–34, 35b

Lord God,
>creator of the living earth and all its creatures,
>calm our troubled souls and anxious spirits
>as we contemplate your wisdom.

We pause from busy schedule and self-imposed fussy bustle,
>to wonder at the rhythms of nature,
>where sea meets shore in easy caress and incessant pounding;
>>stone to sand, shell to grain,
>moving, green to clouded grey, blue to sparkling foam,
>>lull then crash, lull then crash,
>>crest to trough and back;
>>turning tide twice today; never tiring,
>>permanently changing, changing to permanence,
>wind-textured, freshly smelled on breeze or storm,
>>taste of salt the same as tears;
>>living space for bird and fish,
>>all manner of creatures,
>>dependent, independent,
>>hunter and hunted — food for all.

Threatened by heavy-handed human folly
>and a back-turned God dismayed at greed,
>re-created by a new spirit breathing over dying waters.

God, today, caress us with renewing spirit,
>spirit-textured wisdom that gives origin, rescue, sustenance;
God, today, caress us with renewing spirit,
>amidst our changing permanence
>crestfallen and calm,
>our crash and lull,
>our moving, our cloud, our sparkle.

So we bless you, Lord God, and we are blessed.

In the name of the Giver of spirit-wisdom,

AMEN.

PSALM 8

Sovereign Lord,
      we listen for the wise child within,
      who still wonders at your glory
           beyond the glory we see in the heavens.

We marvel and long for that early innocence
      incapable of cultivating enemies within and adversaries without.

We yearn to recapture juvenile surprise and astonishment
      at the grandeur of your days
      and the splendor of your nights.

           Yellowed moon casting silver shadow,
           a milky way splayed against dark sky,
           pinpricks of brilliance varying in intensity,
           twinkling distances beyond imagination,
           time delayed but present.

Sovereign Lord,
      who encompasses every dimension,
      yet can think small enough to think
           "I" and "me" and "we" and "us,"
you draw us up to angel status
      and graciously give us privilege and responsibility
           to co-convene as guardians of the earth,
      and labor for a just sustaining of life,
      and a fair distributing of earth's means.

Sovereign Lord, Father, Son and Spirit,
      creator, created, creating,
      create a willing spirit in us, we pray.

In the name of the One who speaks for creation,

AMEN.

PSALM 46

Lord God, our puny, sometimes awful, strength
    evokes morbid fascination,
    captures us, maybe imprisons us.

For we have enough power to fool ourselves into self-sufficiency.
We treat every experience as problem for solution.
We use knowledge mechanically to cause effect, and affect cause.
We dull our imagination in the service of efficiency.

Lord God —
    What window do you open
        when you offer refuge and strength?
    What light shines
        when we switch to fearlessness as our mode of speech?
    What resources are let loose when your power is undammed
        and we are flooded with glory?

For surely we need your refuge and strength;
    we need your new language to enlighten our day;
    we need a baptism of your glory to lift our mundaneness;
for in our confessional times we admit to unreal claims of self-generated,
    grandiose strength, in a fearful world beyond control.

Still the earth trembles,
    and even though we measure it, we cannot control it.
Still the nations fight, and totter, and maintain uneasy peace,
    and we read of it, but it all goes violently on — a life of its own.
Still our children live in contorted social circumstances
    seeking a way of contentment and fulfilment beyond survival,
    and they seem beyond our influence.

Remind us again to be still, to stop our restless striving,
    and live at least for this hour acknowledging our weakness,
    leaning on your well-proven help,
        within the holy city of your and our imaginings,
    in a world of warless trustfulness,
        where it is you, Lord God, exalted in this congregation.

AMEN.

PSALM 33:1–12

A new song, a new song —
Sing a new song, so you say;
    not an old song, not a familiar song,
    not a common, known, or routine repetition song,
but a new song.

A song unfamiliar to us,
    an uncommon song of unaccustomed rhythms and accents.

Lord God, is this an invitation to us,
    or is it for someone else?
Do you call us to praise and rejoice,
    to make melody and play,
or is it another people called to sing?
Perchance it is us you are addressing,
    and perchance you may find us reluctant learners.

But you are the conductor, upright and faithful,
    beating the tune of righteousness and justice,
        in steadfast love.
And you call us to a congruence,
    a matching, a pairing,
    with reciprocal uprightness, faithfulness,
        righteousness, and justice.

That's the song.
It is a new song.
For we normally sing discordant songs of frustrated plans,
    and counsel without harmony.

But in this hour we gladly sing the song, the new song,
    and perchance its melody may linger through today,
        even into tomorrow
    so we and our world may learn a line of praise.

In the name of the One who sang the song well,

AMEN.

PSALM 116:1–2, 12–19

Lord God —
Who is this one who loves you?
Who is she so intimate that you attentively listen?
Who is he so bold that he dares to speak expectantly? And constantly?

Could she be here among us?
Could he be one of our worship companions?
Could it be me, the one sitting in my seat, occupying my space?

If it is me,
    what shall I return to you, Lord?
How shall I respond,
    to bring to the point of what I could be?

I will begin where it all began.
The vows of baptism are my vows,
    and here in the presence of all these people,
    I will continue to restate them,
        and relive them,
        and relate them to my unfolding life with others.

And the covenant of sacrifice and blessing
    I will share in the presence of the people,
    with whole heart and full intention
        to live the life of the baptized
    and to commune with the other guests at table.

Lord God, support your servants, we pray;
    loosen the bonds that restrict us
    and make us one-eyed and argumentative.

We call on your name
    and for your glory,

AMEN.

PSALM 86:1–10, 16–17

We have heard it a thousand times, O Lord,
    and we come to hear it again.
We have heard you have the capacity to save.
We believe you have the capacity to save us.
We urge you to act.
We press you to intervene in a way
    consistent with your character, inconsistent with ours;
for we are not gods.

Only you are God, and there is none like you,
    who does great things,
    who majors in impossibilities,
    who stirs wonder in us.

This is our plea:
release from the power of personal behavior that shames us,
emancipation from the powers that contort our lives,
freedom to act in ways reflecting gospel talk.

Do you hear, O God?
Because when you hear,
    and act the impossible on our behalf,
    then we are more free to praise, and pray,
        and collaborate with you in covenantal life;
    free from the insidious powers that divert us,
        and suck up our resources;
    free to attend to justice in our homes,
        community of faith, and nation.

God, break the powers, we pray,
    even the warring, oppressive, appalling powers within us,
        and save us for life.

In the name of the Life-giver,

AMEN.

PSALM 13

Lord God, we come Sabbath by Sabbath,
     desperately hoping for a breakthrough into satisfying
fulfillment.

How long must we come?
We seek to be faithful,
     but we question your faithfulness.

We are disabled, incapacitated, impotent;
     we feel disqualified, marginalized, helpless —
     and it is your fault!

For you are the only one who can act for us.
We know, because we have ventured into self-improvement programs
     and "how to" books
     and seductive ideologies,
     and they do not work;
     they fail, they fall crumpled, outside their promise.

Only you can act,
     so when will you intrude into our hope-abandoned,
          nerve-vacated life?
Consider and answer us, O Lord our God!

Because it is urgent, for your sake and for ours;
     for our impotence suggests yours;
     our lack of nerve infers yours;
     our incapacity hints at yours;
and the enemy prevails.

Now we trust you, the giver of abundant steadfast love.
Now we rejoice, for you deliver salvation.
Now we sing,
     for you come with bountiful forgiveness,
     reinstating us as covenantal partners.

AMEN.

PSALM 45:10–17

How can we entertain your being in our midst, Lord God?
How can we make this hour an occasion befitting your presence?

We will forget our immediate concerns
    and celebrate your life among us.
We will escape our anxious busyness
    and rejoice in an hour's joyful freedom.
We will fade out our failures
    and join the company of praise-makers.

We bring our gifts;
we bring our best hopes;
we bring our voice, our song, our word;
we bring our capacity for silence.

We meet your giftedness;
we hear your hopes for you and us;
we hear your speech, your song of harmony,
    your word to us;
we enjoy the silent communing of lovers.

That you should notice us, we are grateful;
that you should engage us, we are excited;
that you should woo and court us, we are overwhelmed;
that you desire a permanent fruitful liaison, we are overcome.

God, Lord God, God of love, lover God,
    in the hour, we come as close as we can
        and revel, rest, nestle,
    in your care-full arms.

AMEN.

PSALM 119:105–112

Lord God, we look to you through love and law,
    we seek you through true love and Torah.

We often over-balance one way or the other,
    cherishing love, and light on instruction,
    or diminishing love, and heavy on teaching.

We compensate by counterweights,
    over-polite, while mean in spirit,
    over-attentive here, but ignoring there,
    kindly charming in public, but coldly calculating in private.

Lord God, we have yet to find the place of poise,
    the mix of love and law
    devoid of vacillation when convenient.

We settle in your presence, with praise and adoration,
    and we settle in your presence with learner's heart.
We dwell in your place of worship with devotion and thanksgiving,
    and we dwell in your place of worship with disciple's readiness.
We pause here in communion with gratitude and benediction,
    and we pause here in communion with student's ear.

So, Lord God,
    instruct us in the speech of love,
    teach us in the language of justice,
    infiltrate this ready heart
        with honesty of thought and purity of motive,
        free of vacillation and unprincipled pragmatism.

Then your guidance is not forgotten,
    and learning becomes our way of life,
    and loving becomes our life's way,
    and we happily, enjoyably live another day.

In the name of the One who intuitively knew how,

AMEN.

PSALM 139:1–12, 23–24

Lord God,
     if you should search me
     if you should test me
you will find a wicked way, an evil thought, a questionable motive.
You will find it; yes, you will. We know.

Would you wish to persist in this love relationship?
     Is the partnership in jeopardy?
     Is the covenant revoked?
For that is what we deserve.

Yet your search is for lostness, not for conviction;
     your discerning is for caring, not for ostracizing;
     your testing is for purifying, not for exposing fault.
And that is too wonderful;
     far more than we could expect from others.

Hemmed in to prevent fraying,
     hand laid on and not abandoned,
     known and not forgotten
        — too wonderful.

We live our lives in your total environment,
     never orphaned, always in reach
     of word, encouragement, forgiveness.
No hiddenness can survive your penetrating eye,
     no bashfulness puts us out of reach.

It's too wonderful.
And we praise you.

Lead us, Lord God, away from life's dead ends
     and lead us into paths of continuing completeness.

In the name of the One who made it,

AMEN.

PSALM 105:1–11, 45b

Lord God,

    all offspring of Abraham,

    all issue of Isaac,

    all of Jacob's line,

    all who stand in the faith tradition,

    all covenant linked and cousins thereof,

    all within the thousand generation span,

    all — without exception,

    all come to pray and praise and recite the story.

So that,

    all potential relatives,

    all unfamiliar with the faith tradition,

    all as yet uncovenanted,

    all lost outside the generations

        may hear, and wonder, and marvel,

        at such persistent life-giving promise.

Lord God,

    give us the courage to discover our story,

    to acknowledge our roots,

    to search out and put into speech

        your place in our history,

        your influence through family,

        your engagement with our story,

        your transformative claim on our lives,

    so that we can say with our lips,

    and sing with our tongue,

    and rejoice in our hearts,

        of your wonderful works,

        the peculiar turns of life presented to us,

        the miracles that surprise us.

Then all may know of their inheritance,

    all may rejoice in their belonging,

    and all may thank their creator.

Praise the Lord!

AMEN.

PSALM 17:1–7, 15

Lord God,
>without boasting we come;
>with humility and void of puffery
>we stand before you.
We wish you to hear our call.

In our best moments we have remained true to you.
We have given of our time, our gifts, our goods.
We have been constant in attending to your place in the world.
We have built up your commonwealth
>and therefore your name in the community.
We have avoided violence and made for peace.
We have been true to our vows and reached beyond our capabilities,
>following the way of faith.

We remind you, Lord, we are not boasting or currying favor.
We are simply stating our disappointment:
 — that things have not always gone well for us,
>even though we are your children,
>apple-eyed children,
 — that your enemies seem to do better than we
>in their happiness, freedoms, wealth,
 — that violence does seem to pay
>and crookedness often works to advantage.

We remind you, Lord,
>our prayer is no conditional plea or ultimatum.
We simply put our case to you
>and ask for your ruling,
>your reordering, your reconstructing our perceptions.
And tomorrow we will awake,
>still your disciples
>still faithful followers
>still seeking your likeness.

In the name of the One who is like you,

AMEN.

PSALM 105:1–6, 16–22, 45b

Lord God, we have a story in our book
    of a boy dreamer with colored coat,
    a lad who invited sibling wrath,
    a young man framed in a political sex scandal,
    a man who endured harsh injustice.

We have a story in our book of a prisoner, interpreter of dreams,
    a captive plucked from jail,
    detained until released by a troubled head of state.

We have a story in our book of a dreamer become wily politician,
    a foreigner become rescuer of a nation,
    the youngest become savior of a family.
What a story! What a tale to tell!

And we have a story in our book of you, Lord God,
    the concealed player,
    the powerful imperceptible One,
    the shadowed shaper of history.
You remind us that dreams are windows on an alternative world,
    that visions are doorways to new life,
    that hopes are promptings for new choices.

So when our dreams, and visions, and hopes
    coincide with your concealed, imperceptible,
        shadowed, powerfully shaped play in history,
then both we and you enter unimaginable freedom,
    and whole fulfilling communion.

So we seek your strength continually;
    we diligently search for your presence.
We remember, tell, recite, rehearse, relive
    the amazing stories of liberation.
And we give thanks.

In the name of One imprisoned, then set free,

AMEN.

PSALM 133

Lord God,
>the psalm descends sweetly on our wearied selves;
>a pleasant balm for a heavy heart.

When we expend so much energy
>on keeping the saints of the faith community
>>from tearing each other's throats out,
>or keeping a work force in creative vigor
>>and not destructive tension,
>or keeping our offspring as sisters and brothers
>>and not enemies;

so the psalm descends sweetly on our fretful selves.

We come, dragging lives in convulsive spasm;
we come, tugging lives cramped and aching;
we come, lugging lives of irritating timidity.

And we come to hear a psalm descending sweetly
>on our disquieted selves.

No anxious calculating
no weary computing
no anguished analysis.
Pure precious gift, alluring, enticing,
>evocative of charm that calms our fear
>>and soothes our troubled souls.

Lord God, descend in ordained blessing
>on these gathered today
>with the balm of this psalm to charm us
>>into union with you and each other.

In the name of the One who calls us to be one,

AMEN.

PSALM 124

Lord God,

    can we join Israel and say with any integrity
    "We are grateful you are on our side,"
    because we have sided with others too often?

Is there anything noble in trusting our personal pedigree?
Is there any virtue in leaning on the school we went to,
    to forge our way through life?
Is there any righteousness in claiming moral high ground?
What excellence in having the correct accent?
What credit in living in the preferred suburb?
What merit in belonging to the socially rewarding club?

None, none, none. Three times, none.
For no one offers protection,
    no one gives refuge,
    no one acts as guardian,
except you, Lord God.

For we are a vulnerable people among vulnerable people,
    a precarious people in jeopardy,
    an exposed people in hazardous circumstances.
But we are a people who know our God,
    a people in conversation with you, Lord God,
    a people pondering our connectedness with you, Lord,
        creator of all our being.

So when alone-ness slams the door,
    we are not alone;
when against-ness shuts us up,
    we have one who is for us and not against us;
when apart-ness tears at our being,
    we are in discourse with a faithful one.

Our help is in the name of the Lord
    who made heaven and earth.

AMEN.

PSALM 105:1–6, 23–26, 45c

Lord God,
>   as foreign people in foreign lands, we look to you for blessing.

As our newly born ones, we ask your blessing on our babies,
>   learning foreign ways in hostile, dangerous places.

As our new school entrants, we ask your blessing,
>   leaving protective parents' home for new social contacts.

As our adolescents, we ask your blessing,
>   living in a foreign body of hormones cut loose
>   and another gender to cope with.

As a new worker or nonworker, we ask your blessing,
>   facing uncertainty, competitive hostility, and broken dreams.

As a new parent, we ask your blessing,
>   coping with the helpless for which we are entirely responsible.

As a midlifer, we ask your blessing,
>   caring for generations both ways,
>   preparing to say goodbye to both.

As a re-entrant into the workforce, we ask your blessing,
>   contending with hostility and patronization.

As a retiring one, we ask your blessing,
>   giving up a long work pattern for an as-yet-unknown life.

As an end-lifer, we ask your blessing,
>   encountering an uncharted mystery ahead.

Lord God, we look for your blessing — and it is urgent.
For some babies die;
>   some children are forever consigned to the lower stream;
>   some adolescents take their own life;
>   some are condemned to a life of no work;
>   some new parents beat their child;
>   some midlifers buckle under pressure;
>   some work re-entrants suffer under power brokers;
>   some retirees die too early;
>   some seniors have not yet fulfilled their dreams.

Therefore, God, remember miraculous deeds once done, and redo them;
>   remember faithful presence,
>   and become again faithfully present;
>   remember kindly judgments, and reimpose them.

We urgently seek your strength, O God; then we can give thanks.

AMEN.

PSALM 149

Lord God,
> today we will praise you,
> today we sing our song of adoration,
> today we celebrate whose we are,
>> sustained by our Maker.

Yet we know the reality of history, and it grieves us;
> For our forebears fought for their faith;
> our ancestors were forced to flee oppressors;
> our mothers and fathers were killed by tyrants.

So two-edged swords come easily to hand,
> and vengeance is close to the surface,
> and the binding of despots is language readily rehearsed
> — for those who remember.

Today in our praise, we remember.

So we act for those still fighting, fleeing, dying:
— those disenfranchised;
— those disadvantaged;
— those where justice has been raw and harsh.
And we act on those who perpetuate unbridled power:
— those who have no notion of neighborliness;
— those who will not remember,
> so seek an ever-accumulating present;
— those who skew justice in their favor.

Lord God,
> whose interest and delight is in seeing us love the neighbor,
> we fulfill our praise this day
> by interceding and acting for neighbors broken,
>> neighbors on the margins,
>> neighbors silent and oppressed.

In the name of the One broken, marginal, and silent,

AMEN.

PSALM 114

Lord God,
> what God are you?
Who are you that staggers an empire, and establishes a disordered tribe?
Who are you that totters a kingdom,
> and constitutes a new community?
Who are you that leaves an oppressive realm ragged,
> and weaves a ragged people into new communion?

For our book tells us
> the oppressive empire staggered, tottered, was left ragged,
> and your faithful people were
> established, constituted, woven together.

You made to flee the sea of permanence;
You halted the interminably running river;
You shook to molehill-size the mighty mountain;
You changed the established hills to minor ripples.

What a laugh!

For now, for us,
> every permanence is up for questioning;
> every interminable process is in for interruption;
> every mountain is surmountable;
> every establishment may be dislodged.
And you, God — it is your doing;
For now, for us, by your miracle of intervention,
> permanence has lost its formidable power;
> interminable process may proceed no more;
> the insurmountable is now surmountable;
> the establishment is now challengeable.

It's like rock turning to water
> and flint sparkling into springs.

Thanks be to God!

AMEN.

PSALM 105:1–6, 37–45

Lord God,
> it is all gift, amazing gift.

All we have and all we are is astonishing gift;
> so we will sing your praises.

You brought our forebears out of weighted oppression
> and you bring us out of burdened past.

You enriched our ancestors in the faith,
> and you enrich us with sufficiency.

You protected our Hebrew parents,
> saving them through each stumble,
> and you protect us in our stumbling.

You give enough light for our next step;
You provide enough food for today
> and adequate water for life;
All because of your remembered promises
> to our faith father and mother, Abraham and Sarah.

Remembered, chosen ones we are,
> in the family of faith.

So we sing your praises;
> we glory in your glory;
> we remember because you remember.

And now we would remember whose we are,
> and pledge to behave in ways
> > consistent with your guided instruction,
> as given us by our faith forebears.

In the name of our chief mentor we pray,

AMEN.

PSALM 78:1–4, 12–16

Lord God,
> we indulge today in giving word to your making a new world;
> we construct a fresh life framework
>> viewed from your perspective;
> we renovated the old picture
>> with a new word picture of transformed life.

We acknowledge our place in the generations;
We are receivers, acquiring our materials from generations who knew you
> and knew how to behave as God-knowers;
We are givers, passing on our constructs,
> understandings, patterns of behavior
> as God-knowers, to a new generation.

We act between generations, not commanding absolute claim on the truth,
> but taking a given,
> remoulding it for the present,
> and passing it on for others to grapple,
> as they interpret your word in their circumstance.

For our part, we search for
— the old sayings
— the ancient perceptions of truth
— how our mothers and fathers lived lives of faith.
For our part, we reflect on how we got here
— the safe passages through terrifying possibilities,
— the people and circumstances that nurtured and sustained us,
— the passing of minor and major miracles that gave us life.
For our part
— we utterly reject today's stagnant present;
> with no acknowledgment of past and no responsibility for future,
— we consciously embrace a new and always changing world,
> transformed by your fresh new word,
— we deliberately step away from center,
> step down from the pinnacle of God space,
>> and offer you our worship and praise.

In the name of the only One equipped to be there,

AMEN.

PSALM 19

Lord God,
> each day a new book is placed in our hands;
> from the opening of our eyes each morning
>> to our closing exhausted evening slumber,
> a new story unfolds
>> — the same as yesterday, but different,
>> — similar to last year, but one step forward,
>> — as normal as it ever was, but a new normality.

But we won't read the book
— too mundane, we say, too repetitive, too uneventful.
We opt for the sensational, the passionate, the scandalous;
> the matters we can get our small heads around;
> the matters that seduce us
> into glorying in others' misdemeanors
> and masking our own.
We avidly read the press, listen to the avalanche of radio speech,
> watch truncated bytes on a screen.
But we don't read the large, fascinating, sustaining, dependable picture
> offered daily,
>> speaking of your glory and saving power.

Lord God,
> divert our eyes away from the captivating useless,
> toward the words of disciplined freedom.
For the hand that writes the wondrous universe,
> also writes the words for living.
And we need to hear them;
> for our plight is desperate,
> our communities are dangerous,
> and our responses are contracting
> into isolated anti-neighborliness.
We are dying in grief,
> pretending we are living in laughter.
We need your word to inform our words,
> and the meditations of our hearts,
>> Redeemer God.

AMEN.

PSALM 106:1–6, 19–23

Lord God, we have a confession to make.
We don't want you.
We don't want you to act in our lives.
We don't want you to act in our lives —
    any act that may bring change.
We don't want you.

We want to settle for what we can control;
we want to settle for the satisfactions we engender;
we want to exchange the glory of what could be
    with a shame we fabricate.
Then we can fill our days with guilt and counseling,
    avoiding taking responsibility for our own actions.
Then at least we are central and in control.
We don't want you.

We want a world of our making, our gods, and our worship patterns.
We have trained our minds to forget;
We have short-circuited our recall abilities;
We have sabotaged our faith memory banks.
We don't want you.

But we don't want our anger either.
We don't want to suffer for our insubordination;
We don't want to perish for our violation of covenant;
We don't want the responsibility tagged to communal insurrection.
Maybe we want you; maybe we need you.
Who can stand in the breach to divert your annihilating rage?
Who can ward off your consuming anger after confession like that?
Have you a chosen one — one picked out —
    who will defend us against holy fury?
If we are to survive, all is in your hands, O God
 — God of steadfast love, remember?
 — God of goodness, remember?
 — God with the capacity to show favor, remember? — we plead.

For the sake and reputation of the One chosen,

AMEN.

PSALM 99

Lord God,
>   you reign over all the earth
>   and you reign in mystery.

For we think we have you contained.
>   We say "At last we understand";
>   We speak confidently of who you are
>>   and what you expect of humanity;

Then you slip unexpectedly sideways
>   to reveal a new, disturbing part of your character,
>   and we tremble in embarrassment at our last claim to absolutes.

How could we be so sure?

Lord God
you comfort us with your solid reliable presence,
you disturb us with your demand for liberation of the oppressed,
you surround us with love engendering well-being,
you disarrange our carefully planned lives with calls to justice,
you content us with your silent peaceful serenity,
you unsettle us with perplexing challenges for fairness
>   among the world's peoples.

We cannot get a handle on you;
>   only a wisp at worship,
>   a tentative string, a covenant cord,
>   a touch of trust, a word spoken through priest and prophet.

But at least in our cry there is your answer;
the heartfelt passionate cry is matched by sure answer:
sometimes silence
sometimes forgiveness
sometimes punishment.

So we will continue to worship here.
We come, tenaciously clinging to you, Lord God,
>   mysterious but specific in encounter.

In the name of the One chosen to speak for you, to us,

AMEN.

PSALM 90:1–6, 13–17

Lord God,
> we come into your presence at this hour of worship.

We come with special language,
> distinct speech, odd turn of phrase, peculiar discourse.

We come because we have learnt a wisdom
> that recognizes gifted belonging
> devoid of isolating homelessness.

We know to whom we belong, so we are confident to speak.

And speak we shall, because our time is short
> and the earth's dust will soon return to reclaim us,
> our lives will soon turn to forgotten dreams,
> the flush of morning life will turn us into faded evening shadow.

Listen, Lord God!

You turn! We can't.
You have pity,
> because self-pity destroys us.

You satisfy us,
> because self-satisfaction brings on smug mediocrity.

You make us glad,
> because our self-gladdening smudges our neighbor.

You open the window on your favor,
> because our attempts at procuring favor are bent.

Lord God, timeless and distant,
come, we pray, and demonstrate your timeliness,
> your rootedness with your covenant people.

Rouse yourself from indifference
> and meet our frustrated attempts at self-saving.

Rouse yourself, we pray,
> so that our work will engender real fruitfulness in your world

> for your sake and for ours,

AMEN.

PSALM 107:1–7, 33–37

Lord God,
>	five youths steal a car;
>	they crash it down a bank;
>	one is seriously injured and four die.

When Torah is broken the world begins to fall apart.
When your instruction is violated our whole world is in jeopardy.

Is it your terrible sovereign freedom that sometimes works against us?
Is it that our behavior influences the process of history and the course
>		of nature?

Does wickedness really turn rivers into desert,
>	and springs into thirsty ground,
>	and fruitful land into salty waste?

God, we are nonplussed.
We are tossed between your unfettered generosity,
>	and what looks like a retributive meanness of spirit.

Except our behavior is the one factor in the equation
>	over which we have some control
>	— we think.

Lord God, forgive us, we pray, for practices that usurp your law;
>	pardon us, we plead, for conduct that violates your instruction;
>	excuse us, we beg, for behavior that infringes your teaching.

We cry out to you;
>	we seek release from our trouble,
>	and deliverance from distress,
>	and motivation to follow in your ways.

We want to live in harmony with you, your Torah,
>	and the world you so generously give.

So find peace with our neighbor
and peace in our selves.

In the name of One who forgives,

AMEN.

PSALM 78:1–7

Lord God,
> schooled as we are in the faith of wonderless, knowing science,
> we find it difficult to admit your life, your influence, your power,
>> in our daily discourse.

Seduced as we are by the language of myth,
> it seems naive to suggest you act
>> in specific ways with particular people.

Immersed as we are in the politics of power and violence,
> attention is easily diverted into present defenses and current fear.

Inundated as we are with the pressure to consume,
> we become pliable in the hands of persuaders
>> peddling scarce commodities.

What do we have to teach our children?
With what do we inform them?
How do we correct them?
What proper nurture can we offer?

Lord God, we must slough off the present absolutes,
> and open our eyes to the parables
>> and hidden sayings of our faith walk.

Teach us to reflect on your ways with us,
> so we have something to tell.

Inform us of your interpretation of life,
> which offers alternatives to science, myth,
>> violence, and consumerism.

Correct our perceptions of life,
> so the language of wonder, surprise, astonishment, and amazement
>> have awe-full currency.

Then we will speak with our children
> of your startling way among us,
> of your strange, unforeseen alternative patterning of life,
> of your incredible promise and hope given,
>> accountable only in terms of your irrational,
>> unreasoned, mystifying, generous love.

Teach us, O Lord,
> in the name of the One who perceived your moves in life,

AMEN.

PSALM 123

Lord God,
>   we seek the faith of the psalmist,
>   weighed down by taunts of scorn,
>   yet who still looks up in hope for mercy.
For surely our world is bent on tearing down;
>   we hear too readily words of criticism
>   and the brutal language of blame and censure;
>   we hear too seldom the words of approval,
>   and the uplifting language of commendation and praise.
We begin to believe depressing comment, sneer, satire, and abuse
>   are normal,
>   because it forms the basis of political life, family life, entertainment
>   and sport, business life, even personal life.

Lord God, we have not yet learnt your language
>   of high esteem for your creatures.
So we lift up our eyes heavenwards
>   to discover a new schoolroom,
>   an alternative teaching, another option,
>   to the common carping we drown in.

Lord God,
>   shower us with mercy,
>   bathe us in gracious love,
>   clothe us in compassion,
>   cover us in tender liking,
>   enough for us to believe in the new speech-making.
Uplift us with words of worth,
>   upraise us to new levels of praise,
>   hoist us high with songs of gratitude,
>   upheave our heaviness into new light
>   enough to practice this foreign language.

For then the scorn and contempt we are used to will disappear,
>   and our new mother tongue will bring glory to you,
>   and blessing to neighbor,
>   and health to self.

In the name of the One who could talk with affirmation,

AMEN.

PSALM 100

Lord, our God,
      we open these doors to the place of thanksgiving,
      and we open our mouths with praise.
We enter this assembly with praise on our lips,
      and we enter into worship of you, Lord God.

We thank you, we bless your name,
      the name that belongs to the face we seek.

Lord, our God,
      may this place of worship become
            a microcosm of earth's possibility;
      may this assembly become
            a mini-climate for a world's fruitfulness;
      may this slice of time become a model for all time.

For today we celebrate that enduring, imperishable, insuppressible,
      steadfast love toward all people of every generation.

Today we dance in the pasture of your making,
      knowing we are your people
            — not one left out,
            — each included,
            — everyone counted as a belonger.

Today in this hour we touch heaven,
      window in on paradise,
      smell the whiff of perfumed presence.

And today we carry the grand blessing of the hour
      into the week to come
      that our days may be transformed
      because we were here.

In the name of the One whose presence transformed the hour,

AMEN.

Year B

THE YEAR
OF MARK

PSALM 80:1–7, 17–19

We catch you, Lord God, as patient shepherd,
    — knowing by name, leading the lamb.
We catch you as holy cherubim,
    — guarding the word, with flaming sword.
We catch you leading the heavenly host,
    — fearless, courageous, protective, victorious.

We see ourselves on the verge of Christmas preparation
    — frantic, worrying, overcome by strife,
    — fitfully praying, weeping troubled tears of anxiety,
    — enough to make our neighbors wonder at our claims of faith.

Why should you, Lord God of hosts, Holy Lord, Shepherding God,
    why should you take note of us tragic depressives,
        unloved and unlovely?

Unless you are disposed toward us;
Unless you are inclined to care;
Unless you are intent on lively preservation of your image.

We must bank on it.
We must rely on your willingness to save;
We must reckon on your high rate of interest in our well-being.

Who else will restore us?
Who else will turn a kindly face?
Who else will take us by the hand?

Only you, our creator; so to you we plead for life.

In the name of the One at your right hand,

AMEN.

PSALM 85:1–2, 8–13

Let us hear what God the Lord will speak.
Let those who are faithful,
>   those who turn their hearts to God,
>   let them hear the word of God today.

Surely God's salvation is near for those who look constantly.
Surely God's glory will find a place to live, when people seek diligently.

Lord God, we know of your steadfast love, your faithfulness
>   so different from the instant gratification we seek,
>   so different from our ability to decide, then buy,
>>   then suffer disappointment,
>>   when our newly acquired fancy fails to deliver.

We yearn for steady love and faithfulness to surround us.
We yearn for rightness of relationship and peace
>   between ourselves and neighbors.

Lord, may we intercept the kiss of righteousness and peace.
May we be courted and wooed and engaged
>   in this uncommon, beautiful relationship.
May righteousness and peace find consummation within us,
>   and new birth among us this Advent,
>   so that our sin is pardoned,
>   and our iniquity is forgiven
>   and you, Lord, would give us what is good.

In the name of One soon born,

AMEN.

PSALM 126

Lord God, in our reflective moments we know the dream of Advent is
    no flight of fancy
    no vagary of the mind
    no vapor of whim.

The dream of Advent
    excites our imagination
    amazes us with its originality
    enthuses us with its boldness.

The dream of Advent — God with us —
    lifts our speech above the gravity
        and weighted heaviness of mundane discourse, to
    a conversation of joy
    a dialogue of delight
    a communion of gladness.

Lord God, your dream becomes our sparking vision; it
    tips us into laughter
    bursts our souls with unbridled joy
    conceives in us novel imagination.

Because this dream of Advent — God with us —
    has feet on our earth,
    has skin and bone, sinew and muscle,
    hands that touch and eyes that see, twinkle, watch.

The Advent Lord is doing great things among us — God with us —
    turning tears into shouts of joy
    and weeping into newly watered seeds of hope.

Restore us, O Lord.

In the name of the Advent One,

AMEN.

PSALM 89:1–4, 19–26

You made your choice, O God;
>   You anointed and crowned your elect;
>   You promised your strength, and wit, and cunning;
>   You guaranteed your faithfulness and steady love;
>   You gave authority and established
>>   a firm, rock-like, stable relationship
>>   with your selected One.

We remember this One with whom you made covenant;
>   we know from the stories of your preferred One;
>   we keep in mind the One who receives your favor.

From within our managed autonomy and failed self-sufficiency
>   we venture to remind you of our family — your family
>   — the one with established descendants forever
>   — the one that stretches from generation to generation,
>>   to our generation.

We place before you our adoption papers, our certificate of baptism,
>   to impress upon you to whom we belong,
>   encouraging you to retrace the family lines
>>   from the One with whom you once covenanted,
>   right through to our generation.
We are part of the family — the family of Sarah and Abraham
>>   Bathsheba and David
>>   Mary and Joseph
>   and of the child whose birth we celebrate in a few days.
We are part of that family;
>   so may we too not be outwitted by enemies,
>   or humbled by the wicked,
>   or crushed by foes, or struck down by the hateful.
As part of the family, may we too enjoy faithfulness and steadfast love
>   and find exaltation in wearing the new adopted name.

So we cry to you — "Our Father, our Mother!
>   Our God — the rock of our salvation."

In the name of the Elder Brother we pray,

AMEN.

PSALM 96

We sing a new song today.

We sing a song made new
    by the anniversary of Christ's birth.
We sing a new song as angels sang:
    Glory to God in the highest
    and on earth, peace.

We sing a new song, all of us
    even if the rough passage out distorts the sound,
    even if we can't keep the tune;
    we sing a new song.
We sing a new song
    even if it is under our breath in case someone hears,
    even if self-consciousness gets the better of us;
    we sing a new song.

The song made new because
    God is with us.
We sing a new song
    old words
    old tradition
    old story
    new song
because of newness within ourselves.

Newness born when babies are born.
Newness born when Christ is born.
Newness born when our memory and the present meet, and conceive
    new hope
    new life
    God with us.

We sing a new song
    when Christ is born.

AMEN.

PSALM 97

Lord God, whom we acknowledge today
>   we have been assaulted by the reigning gods of our time,
>   we have faced the onslaught of the consumer machine,
>   we have endured the aggression of glossy advertisements.
Our lounges are littered with whims and fancies
>   materialized in gadgets and fashions.
Our Christmas trees twinkle with energy.
Our laden tables groan under abundant disguised sugar, fat, and protein.

And we draw aside to ask, "Who reigns in the earth?"
For the moment, we answer,
>   "It is the Lord."
>   "The Newborn King."
>   "O Holy Child of Bethlehem."
>   "Christ the Redeemer."
>   "The Little Lord Jesus."
>   "Child in the Manger."
>   "God Incarnate and the Virgin's Son."
>   "Word of the Father."

For the moment we burst out with heaven and earth
>   proclaiming his authority
>   endorsing his dynasty
>   testifying to his rule
>   so that all that seems durable,
>   shakes and trembles, collapses and melts,
>   and the Child who seems so vulnerable,
>   holds the hope of the whole world in his body.

"Who reigns in the earth?"
>   The One who promotes righteousness and justice.
May that One be our companion, and that be our song.

In the name of the Song-maker,

AMEN.

PSALM 98

Praise to you, Lord God:

One day of the year
    you remind us again
        of your intrusion into the planet's systems
        of your intervention into the affairs of the nations
        of your infiltration into the concerns of humanity.

One day of the year
    you burst into our self-sufficiency
        with declaration of return from exile
        with announcement of exodus from slavery
        with prophetic word of unimagined newness.

One day of the year
    you interrupt our carefully controlling systems
        with claims over earth and sea
        with prerogative over raging weather
        with authority over seismic movement.

One day of the year
    the world does not serve our strategies.

One day of the year
    the world abandons sensible, patterned, predictable procedure,
    and bursts out in irrational joy.

Because the Lord has come
    God with us
    joy to the world.

Praise to you, Lord God!

AMEN.

PSALM 148

How could you ignore us, Lord God?
How could you put us before the angels
    and the whole heavenly host?

Surely we are more important than sun and moon?
Surely we religious have precedence over shining stars?
Surely we faithful rank above the highest heavens and heaven's waters?

For we wish to praise the name of the Lord.
Weren't we created also?
Weren't we established forever?

Surely we are more important than deep sea monsters?
Surely we religious have precedence over fire and hail,
    snow and frost, and stormy wind?
Surely we faithful rank above wild animals and all cattle,
    creeping things and flying birds?

But you give us our place,
    and put us at the end of the chain of praise.
We are not the initiators.
We are not the maestro conductor of the Hallelujah Chorus.

We join with all other praise-makers
    and hold our particular tune in the cosmic harmony,
    granted dignity and renown,
    called "close to God."

Now we praise you, Lord, our God,
    free of the weight of speaking for creation,
    free to be ourselves
        our true selves
        old and young together.

We praise the Lord!

AMEN.

PSALM 147:12–20

Praise to you, Lord God:
    builder of community,
    strengthener of the binding ties,
    provider of a future,
    peace-maker among those who covenant to belong,
    sustainer of health and well-being.

Praise to you, Lord God:
    commander of the earth,
    director of flurried snow,
    overseer of silent frost,
    chief of wind-driven hail,
    initiator of thaw between peoples,
    moderator of an obedient creation.

Praise to you, Lord God:
    speaker to a receptive people,
    architect to a covenant community,
    word-giver to the inarticulate,
    story-maker for a confused people,
    law-maker for the gracious,
    grace-giver to the lawful.

Praise to you, Lord God:
    who else hears your word,
    and who will live by it?

We hear your word:
we will live by it.

In the name of the One called Word Made Flesh,

AMEN.

PSALM 29

Lord God,
> in a world dedicated to speaking without hearing,
> in an environment addicted to noise without meaning,
> in a culture intent on maiming with deafness,
we need special encouragement to hear your voice.

If it takes thunder to make us attentive,
> then thunder over us;
If it takes a furious wind to capture our imagination,
> then blast about us;
If it takes lightning or earthquake to dazzle the skies,
> call us to account,
> then shake the foundations.

For we have forgotten your glory.
We believe the conversation is confined to earth alone.
We are persuaded the only voice is our voice
> and that heaven has no place and no voice.

Carve through our clamor;
Slice through our slender shouting;
Dismember our troublesome tongue
> so we may hear the inner voice of worship
>> — glory to the Lord
>> — glory to the Lord's name
>> — glory to the Lord in holy splendor;

> and hear the quiet voice of favor
>> — peace upon you
>> — blessing from the Lord
>> — strength to those in worship.

In the name of the Prince of Peace we pray,

AMEN.

PSALM 139:1–6, 13–18

You and me, Lord God.

You are the knower, and I am known.

Who am I, that you are mindful of me?
Who are we, that we are the focus of your so searching attention?
What makes you occupy yourself with such intricate detail?
How is it we are the subject of such penetrating gaze?

Lord God, your probing, your thorough discernment of our being,
     gives us confidence;
         — we are taken deeply seriously
         — worth the careful examination
         — valued in spite of, because of
             all our actions, thoughts, hopes, idiosyncrasies.

Completely known?

God, how can you?
How do you know what questions to ask? what to observe in us?
Unless you are one who knows your self;
Unless you have made a thorough introspection
         — perhaps know what thoughts we are both capable of
         — what ways we might both explore
         — what variety of words we may both utter.

You are the knower; we are the discoverers;
You are the One who nourishes genuine developing and fond relationship;
And you are the One who pushes us beyond knowing,
     toward the wonder of, "I am with you"
         — our only certainty.

In the name of One known to us, Jesus Christ,

AMEN.

PSALM 62:5–12

God, we have searched high and low for satisfaction of soul.
We have championed wealth as a sign of your favor.
We have defended poverty as a measure of godly obedience.
We have admired those of high status
     as the legitimate receivers of life's satisfactions.
We have maintained those of low estate
     as true recipients of blessing.
We have been honest in our quest for wealth.
We have been less than honest in our acquisitiveness.

Our hope for gain is incessant
     whether in shares, lottery, dividends, or gambling,
     whether honestly, or dishonestly,
     in good faith, or faithlessly,
     in fairness, or unfairly.

And you tell us, all that is in vain?

Lord God, how could you!
Our whole life is dedicated to who owes what to whom;
But you say the owed to and the ower are but breath
     — deluded breath at that.
Our whole reputation hangs on the balance of weight being in our favor.
But you say our natural bent is featherweight and still wanting.
Tell us once, twice; tell us a third time, we pray,
     that power is yours, and you dispense a truly satisfying,
     loving, steady relationship;
     as steady as rock and fortress.

From our ambiguous, shifty,
     sometimes magnanimous, sometimes questionable selves,
     we fall silent,
     and wait, in trust for you, alone.

AMEN.

PSALM 111

Not alone, Lord God;
      not alone do we give praise,
      not alone, but in the company of the congregation;
      in public meeting,
      with people we know — fellow believers.
Together we declare your greatness.

In the stories of our people
      we notice your bias toward righteousness.
In the histories handed down
      we observe your mercy toward your creatures.
In the narratives we recite week by week
      we recognize your abundant provision.

You live, you offer, you model
      an alternative to our crippled righteousness,
      a contradiction of our mean mercy,
      a reversal to our restrictive hoarding.

Faithful, upright, truly covenantal, is your work;
      arching over your time, woven in to our time,
      punctuating my time.

That's why we say, "Holy and awesome is your name!"

For those of us who practice faith,
      fear is our reminder not to presume too much on your holy name.
Wisdom counsels us of the danger of your close presence.
Yet we would still praise you.

In the name of the One exemplifying your character,

AMEN.

PSALM 147:1–11, 20c

We praise you, our God.

Is a song of praise fitting in our congregation?
Have we recognized your graciousness?
Do we see the evidence of your building up our fellowship?
And whose task is it to build up the fellowship?
We think it may partly be our responsibility.

Where are the outcasts, the brokenhearted, the wounded?
are they gathered, healed, enfolded?

Lord God, make us true to your calling
      to draw together outcasts in congregation
      to nourish the broken in the assembly
      to bind wounds in communion.

So that each may reach stardom,
      and our praise dazzle you in brightness
      against the backdrop of dark death.

For you are the God who orders stars and seasons,
      and energizes seed, and provides food;
      you are the God who builds the church with the downtrodden,
          the ostracized, the lonely, the isolated.
Your vote is for them, transforming them into welcome companions,
      neighbors, forgers of the family circle;
      and neither the power of political force,
      nor the personality of the beautiful people,
      receive your vote.

So we, the ordinary, who become extraordinary by your presence,
      we praise you
      today and always.

In the name of the One who proclaims the gospel,

AMEN.

PSALM 30

Lord God,
>you have moments of anger
>but lifetimes of goodness.

Because of our sin we deserve lifetimes of your anger
>and moments of your goodness.
But because of your love and grace
>we receive goodness and seldom see your anger

Thank you, Lord God, for your loving kindness.

Lord God,
>we have taken your protection for granted
>and have twisted it to make us think
>we were secure in ourselves.

We are fearful and complain when you become hidden
>and we are tempted to say "There is no God."

Forgive us, Lord God, for believing we are gods,
>closing off ourselves from you,
>cutting the lines of your sustaining life,
>until we become wizened and dry.
Lord God, the One who listens to beggars —
>we beg for your help,
>for we are dying, no longer able to praise you.
Help us, Lord,
>be merciful to us.

Lord, God of joy and dancing,
>because we are made in your image,
>may we reflect your joy, your dance, your song of delight,
>and give you our thanks forever.

AMEN.

PSALM 41

Do you know, Lord God,
>   do you know how devastating it is
>   when people watch you die?
Do you know the loneliness when enemies are waiting
>   to see a disease finally conquer?
Do you know how crushing it is
>   when a trusted friend withdraws to the ranks of distant observer?

Yes, you do.

Do you know what it is
>   when people wish you would go away;
>   wish your name would perish;
>   wish you had never intruded into their world?

Yes, you do.

Do you know the emptiness of comforting words
>   from a mischievous heart?
Do you know the cold kiss of uncaring betrayal?
Do you know destructive gossip from a pseudo-friend?

Yes, you do; our forebears in the faith did it to you.
Yes, you do, Lord God; we have done it to you.

So when we cry to you from our inner, isolated loneliness,
>   you know us full well;
>   and you come to the heart,
>   to cleanse by confession,
>   to render pure by honesty,
>   and uphold by integrity.

Thus, we praise you,
>   God of Israel,

In the name of the One who says "Yes,"

AMEN.

PSALM 103:1–13, 22

Lord God,
>speak with us today,
>that we may then say with the psalmist:
>"Bless the Lord, O my soul,
>and all that is within me, bless his Holy Name."

Lord God,
>the giver, and forgiver, healer, redeemer,
>who showers us with love and mercy;
>without your word to us, our words fall flat, empty, lethargic;
>but with your word in ear, praise comes to life,
>and we say,
>"Bless the Lord, O my soul,
>and all that is within me, bless his Holy Name."

Now buoy us up as the eagle is borne up by the wind,
>as we gather in liturgy today.

Lord God,
>you have acted in history,
>in the history of our community,
>in our personal history.

You have brought us this far by your grace —
>you have not repaid us evil for evil,
>but you have given us love, acceptance, embrace,
>>even when we did not acknowledge it.

You have removed the stumbling block of sin,
>and opened the way for communion with you;
>just as the best of parents love,
>in spite of a child's behavior.

So we in your presence here, today,
>we call this place home,
>because of your grace.

May we revel in it.

In the name of One who loved us,

AMEN.

PSALM 50:1–6

God the Lord,
>   you summon us to wake, to arise, to prepare,
>   to come to worship today.

From the rising sun to its setting, you speak of creation's beauty
>   in community life
>   in fellowship time with friend and neighbor
>   in communion time with the community of faith.

For the moment in this place,
>   you, Lord God, are the judge, the redeemer,
>   who buys us back
>   — the focus, the center, the kingpin, the nurturing mother.

Give us ears to hear your silent voice
>   as we gather for worship:

May your call to covenant be heard again today.
May your word be heard in the words of liturgy today.
May your invitation to life be embraced, not denied.
May your future and our future co-mingle for your freedom and ours.

Teach us to trust
>   to stop reclaiming control
>   to begin placing our lives in your sure love and care
>   to give the care of loved ones to you.

And as the heavens declare your righteousness,
>   enable us to follow suit,
>   and declare our willingness
>   to righteous life
>   to fulfilling life
>   to risky, precarious, surprising life.

In the name of the One who surprised us beyond measure,

AMEN.

PSALM 25:1–10

In trust we come to you, our God.

We are tired of acting as shame-faced faithful.
We are irritated by the gloating mischief of the ungodly.
We are distressed by a society out of touch with you.

We wish to give up debilitating defeat
        and be a learner in your school,
        so that you and we make a difference.

Teach us, we pray, how you view the world,
        how you see humanity,
        your perception of us.

So that we may see each other,
        and humanity,
        for each other.

Remind us again of your kindness and constant love
            that open new ways for us to relate to each other
            — in kindness, and with love.
Covenant-making God,
        help us to keep covenant with you
        and with all your world,
        so that you and we make a difference.

Douse us with humility
        so that we can act with integrity with your world,
        and so follow the path that leads to life.

AMEN.

Psalm 22:23–31

Lord God,
>   you had every right to turn away from us,
>   because we turned from you.
You, who are dedicated to life,
>   could well have given up on us,
>   we who are dedicated to violence and death.
We who forget the community,
>   disregard each other,
>   and neglect even our families,
why should we assume you will remember us?

We who easily turn our attention to ourselves,
>   focus solely on our own concerns,
>   and fervently polish our own souls,
why should we suppose you will keep us in mind?
But it dawns, at long last,
>   that our rampant individualism distorts even our best.
And yet you have not despised us,
>   you have not held us in contempt because of our affliction.

Lord God, in a rare moment of recognition of who we are —
>   people together with all earth's families and nations,
>   people together with all those who have gone before,
>   people together with the congregations that nurtured us,
>   and the congregations within our denomination,
>   and congregations which neighbor us —
>   we admit and declare our commitment
>   to mission in your world.
May our offspring also serve you, Lord God.
May future generations be told by us, of your sovereign power.
May those yet unborn learn your liberating story, from us!
May we be a people whose energy is not sucked up by infighting
>   but dedicated to telling the story of salvation,
>   so that those who seek you will find you,
>   and thus praise the Lord.

In the name of the Afflicted One,

AMEN.

PSALM 19

Lord our God,
>   when our praise is absent,
>   the heavens tell of your glory;
>   when our worship is muted,
>   day and night bear eloquent silent witness
>   to your reputation;
>   when our creed and dogma dies within,
>   the earth cries out in delight.

For the earth knows to whom it belongs,
>   and the heavens peal in gratitude to their Maker.
But we have grown deaf to the joyous laughter of nature
>   and blind to the glad spectrum of day.
To whom can we turn to revive our dulled souls?
Where is a resource for regeneration?
What word do you have, Lord God,
>   that will bring our sagging spirits to life?
With relieved gratitude we note,
>   not only did you create our environment,
>   but you spoke within our bounds in ways that enlighten.

So your instruction opens a window for an imprisoned soul;
your simple tuition appeals to us, the ignorant clever;
your counsel fills an empty joyless heart;
your clarity of vision for us brings sparkle to a dulled eye;
your demand for respect brings tested word of worth
>   to our storehouse of understanding;
your true guidance sets us in right paths.

Our consciousness is shaped by more than wealth
>   or sweet satisfactions.
Our consciousness is shaped by your word in us,
>   and our determination to de-absolutize our petty law.
So may the words of our mouths
>   and the meditations of our hearts
>   be acceptable to you,
>   O Lord, our rock and our redeemer.

AMEN.

PSALM 107:1–3, 17–22

Good Lord, redeemer of those sold out on life,
      gatherer of those flung into society's wastelands —
that your love endures forever, we are profoundly grateful.
Someone will buy us back and reassemble the lost ones.
For our best gratitude, even if doubled,
      hardly expresses our thanks for your unfettered,
      boundless generosity to us
      who so desperately need salvation.

We, too, were sick because of our sinful ways.
We have grown anxious to protect our property
      because we have forgotten it is all gift.
We have grown obnoxiously superior in our efforts to enslave others
      and have forgotten they are our sisters, our brothers.
We have grown desperate in our attempts to control the other gender
      and forgotten they are our companions.
We have grown fearful and dangerously angry
      at those of another sexual orientation
      forgetting each one has a place in God's world.
We have grown nationalistic and narrowly defensive
      and have forgotten we belong to a community of neighbor-nations.
We have grown dismissive of the aged and the young,
      forgetting their wisdom and delightful innocence.
We have grown abusive of, and reckless toward, God's creation,
      forgetting we are stewards, and not masters.

God, we are sick through our sinful ways,
      and we loathe any kind of nourishment,
         any new idea, any surprise
      that may modify our privileged place.
But, near destruction, we cry out;
      in distress we mournfully call.
Heal us; deliver us.
Then we have capacity to thank you, and give the offering due to you.

In the name of the One who offers all,

AMEN.

PSALM 51:1–12

We make a Lenten confession.

Lord, our God, we do not often make heartfelt confession,
>	so we do not often hear your word of mercy and steadfast love,
>	and our not-oftenness makes us believe you may not have mercy.
But fresh, today, we cry out.
Hear us, O God;
>	we have nothing to bring except our desperate selves,
>	we who have chosen a single exclusive line of autonomy.
Broken and abused relationships litter our past,
>	right from our beginnings,
>	which culminate in compounded fractures of relationship with you.

Two things we know:
>	you have said you are a God of mercy;
>	we know our sin.
Will these two strands of knowledge meet?
Will we allow your mercy to impinge on our sin?
Will we allow our sin to be subsumed by your mercy?
And will you notice if we acknowledge our sin before you?

If we truly wish cleanliness, washing, new baptism;
if we truly wish rejoicing, resounding joy;
if we truly wish blotted-out foulness —
>	we have the only choice of throwing ourselves on your mercy.
That we do.
Hear us, O God.
Listen to our plea.

Create, restore, sustain
>	a capacity to begin again,
>	a desire to shed worn-out, ragged, dead-end behavior,
>	a courage to take on conduct which is Spirit-fed.

In the name of the Mercy-giver we pray,

AMEN.

PSALM 118:1–2, 19–29

Lord God, you hold open the gate
     for us to enter into your presence.

You invited us into the place where our prayers are made,
     and where answers are given.

You teach us the way of prayer
     that begins with gratitude and thankfulness,
     because bitter, isolated, or indifferent hearts
     are in no mood to hear your word;
          but thankful hearts hear.

So Lord, our God, today here in this place
speak to our bitterness
penetrate our isolation
overturn our indifference.

Lord God
take my bitterness
take my isolation
take my indifference.
Leave it at the gate, so that my thankful heart
     may have a chance to give you the gratitude due to you.

So, this is the day that you have made —
     may you find rejoicing hearts, glad hearts.

Hearts and minds clear of the gunk that clogs the free flow of life.
Hearts and minds ready to hear you.
Hearts and minds ready to give and receive blessing.
Hearts and minds transformed by love.

We give you thanks, O God, for you are good.
Your steadfast, enduring love is with us all our days.

AMEN.

PSALM 31:9–16

Lord God,
       could it be more desolate?

How could you treat so despicably
       those who love you?
How could you allow shattered bones and rotting flesh
       and disintegrating personhood?
How could you inflict such utter loneliness,
       withdrawing neighbor and friend,
       and imposing scheming saboteurs and assassins?

Alone, God, utterly alone;
in a world of alone people, friendless, neighborless,
       where alone is normal.

Yet —
We are still talking to you, God.
We are here.
We are appealing to your graciousness,
       as one worthy of trust.
We are saying, "You are our God!"

Face the lonely ones;
look at them, we pray;
see their plight.

"You are our God,"
       so act in this lonely neighborhood, lonely nationhood,
       and save us all.

In the name of One who knew loneliness,

AMEN.

PSALM 22

Who is happy on this Friday, Lord God?
Who could possibly relish a Friday like this Friday?
Some do; some are happy.
Mockers are; too certain, too banal, too sure of their rightness,
    too ready with their verbose, cynical advice.
Bulls are, fearful strong bullies,
    too weak to curb their unbridled power.
Dogs are, lunging, savaging, worrying,
    doggedly persisting with their deathly terrier task.
The croupier's precursor is,
    throwing dice for worthless gain.
What a Friday, where only hate was happy,
    marring every Friday since, exhausting week's end.
Lord God, must it be this way?

What kind of forsaking drives you to forsakenness?
What kind of despised scorning impels you to suffer scorn?
What melting dust makes you return to death dust?
Are we so forsaken that you meet our forsakenness?
Are we so scorn-despised by heaven that you have taken on our despising?
Are we so near dust to dust that you return to remake us?
O God, on this groaning Friday,
    where cries emerge from dried throat,
    and death's jaws know no bounds,
we sit and wait, watching, helpless,
    remembering our once praise,
    remembering our once-nurturing mother God,
    remembering our once close communion
    – sister and brother in joyful exaltation.
We sit and wait, watching, helpless,
    with ready vow to do justice
    to tell your good word, to serve you to our utmost.
But, on this Friday
    all power for life is gone
    and only you, Lord God, can act.

AMEN.

PSALM 118:1–2, 14–24

Lord God, we arise and feed,
    we gather, stand, sing,
    we sit, pray, and praise
on the day you made;
you carefully crafted it for celebration.
You fashioned it to send the rejoicing body of jubilant believers
    into the world's arena.

For on this day we shout out,
    "I shall not die, but I shall live!"
    because the one we pinned our hopes on,
    the one we pinned our sins on,
    has now come out and cried out,
    "I shall not die, but I shall live!"

It was finished, my God; my God, forsaken into your hands
    the spirit of our last and only hope.
Passive as stone, laid to rest.

But the unforeseen has happened,
    the unimaginable has sprung upon us,
    the undreamt of has burst into new story.
And it is all your marvelous doing.

Thanks be to you, O God.

Now we live with our living Lord,
    to go out the gates, a community dispersing
    into a world battered with the broken language of death,
    yet to hear the new vernacular of life.

May your steadfast love punctuate our vocabulary,
    may every word uttered be a word of life,
    so the world may share the glad songs of victory.

In the name of the Risen One,

AMEN.

PSALM 133

Lord God, once more the Christ tribe gathers,
        and gathers in our town
        and gathers in our nation
        and the sun that bids us rest is waking gatherers
                in nations westerly.

As in heaven, your will of blessed unity be done on earth
        amidst your gathered tribes.

Because our abundant blessing is dependent on blessed unity,
        ordained by you,
        and borne by all who wear the name "Christian."

But in our world, even amongst gatherers,
        the quiet dew of blessing has missed,
        and there's a drought on unity.

We exploit our given differences
        in the name of the natural order of powers,
and we institute manufactured differences
        in the name of competitive advantage,
and blind ourselves to the tragic consequence
        of diminished life for all.

Forgive us for such witless stupidity.
May each become an oil-bearer,
        lubricating the places of unnecessary abrasiveness
        between generations,
        within generations,
        between interest groups,
        between variations of perception
                within your covenanted people.
Only then your ordained blessing will flourish for all.

In the name of the One who taught "Your will be done,"

AMEN.

PSALM 4

Lord God, you say you are a God for those who suffer injustice;
     then be a God for sufferers today, we pray.
The honor of your people is at stake,
     as is your honor — you whom we name as our God.

We have said we side with justice
     and are against liars,
but we ponder on our forebears' perpetuation of injustice
     to their shame.

So our strident plea for a hearing
     mellows into a pleading forgiveness.

For we who say, "O that we might see some good!"
     need your enlightening in our lives,
     that we may do some good, and give up lying,
     and abandon our calculating for advantage.
Then we may lie down to sleep in peace,
     resting in your careful safety for all.

Hear our prayer, we humbly ask,
in the name of the Honorable One,

AMEN.

PSALM 23

Shepherd Lord,
>   in a world of predators,
>   shepherds are a heaven-sent necessity.

In a culture of unsatisfied consumers and scarcity by design,
>   not to lack is a precious commodity.
In a society rattled in rat-racing,
>   resting with satisfying enoughness restores our rhythms.

Shepherd Lord,
>   in a world of mucky turbulence,
>   still, clear water refreshes nervous hearts.

In a culture designed to displace souls,
>   restoration is an unbelievable offer.

In a society of tilted, contorted topography,
>   a visionary path — steady and purposeful — dissipates anxiety.

Shepherd Lord, our named guide,
>   who will not shrink from darkest ventures,
>   your fearlessness spills over our fearfulness
>   dissipating the power of evil,
>   supporting us in our apprehensions.

So we are ready to attend your banquet,
>   perfumed and cup-filled.

Let us forget the enemy;
>   for our days mingle with guests called goodness and mercy,
>   and, Lord, your house is our home.

God, at home for our life-time,

AMEN.

PSALM 22:25–31

Lord, our God,
>   on the far side of death
>   on the other side of a vacant tomb
>   in the world of resurrection,
we would briefly settle.

For this hour
>   we live in Easter habitat with fellow adventurers,
>   a congregation of praise-makers, and justice-seekers.

May our brief settlement in this Easter hour
>   be a remembering of all nations and families.
May the dismembering on our side of death
>   be re-collected into a community of Easter worshipers.
May the community of saints, our faith forebears,
>   gather with us in the world of Easter hour,
>   joining in praise and vow-bound, hopeful justice.

So that you, Lord God, are properly proclaimed,
>   and we are intent on hope-full life,
>   reflecting the Easter world to our children,
>   our neighbors, our workmates,
>   who are yet to discover the window of entry
>   into the world called resurrection.

Hear our prayer,
in the name of the One Adventurer gone before,

AMEN.

PSALM 98

Not with speechless assumed acknowledgment,
  but with voice of praise;
Not with muzzled gratitude,
  but with cries of joy;
Not with tongue-tied thanksgiving,
  but with articulated gladness;
Our song, new for worship, peals throughout the earth.

We hold our tongue no longer,
  for righteousness, steadfast love, and faithfulness
  abound for attentive watchers,
  and the whole earth witnesses the praise of grateful people saved.

So, today, our music notes no bounds.
Chord and harmony sing praise to our God;
  tune and melody dance to our God;
  tenor and alto, soprano and bass,
    pitch notes of playfulness in concert to our God.
Tone deaf and rough passage out
  key in to a consonance of sound in joyful noise.
Offbeat syncopates sharps, flats, and naturals,
  between measured beat of life-giving rhythm.
Major and minor among us compliment our living Lord.
Because you, Lord, have come — joy to the world!
Easter wraps us in life-giving delight.
For what was sure dead now lives;
  the dirge has turned to mighty chorus;
  the requiem becomes a rousing hymn;
  the lament is lost to cantata of cathedral proportions.

Christ has risen!

AMEN

PSALM 1

Lord God,
Torah talk is unfamiliar to our ears.
Obedience to your instruction sounds hard.
We are too used to listening to ourselves
    and to noting the advice of "How to" books.
We are adept at calculating our way through life,
    wedded to a points system even in our families.

Easy pragmatism is our common creed,
    and self-preservation our chief motivation.

Lord God,
    deliver us from center place,
    and gather us around your word,
    so that your fixed reference point
        will hold our scribed arc in ordered sweep.

May our lifeline draw strength from the freshness of Torah life;
    May the springs of covenantal law
        flow through our consciousness;
    May our barren lives give way to fruitful abundance,
        as you seed our days in companionable watchfulness.

Because we notice, as you notice,
    that lightweight lives without Torah ballast
        are easily blown away,
    that no defense is offered in the face of life's tests,
    that sin shows its bleak color where righteousness flourishes.

So in our choosing, Lord God, this day we abandon perishing by neglect
    and choose words spoken in constructive love.

AMEN.

PSALM 104:24–34, 35b

Lord God, we come into your house of freeing Spirit,
> with no need to fear,
> no cause for anxiety,
> at ease in your presence.
We come into your designated worship home,
> reflecting on the vastness you have created,
> the variety you sustain,
> the threat you vanquish.

For in the great wide deep,
> small and large, furious and passive,
> find their place only in reference to you.

So on this day of gifts we proclaim
> we live in a world of giftedness.

In this hour of worship we announce
> we have no misgivings, no timidity, no disquiet,
> for we live for the hour in your wonderful world.

Lord our God, giver of gifts
> we are in awe at your sustaining ways;
> every living thing is dependent on you
> — your presence
> — your breath
> — your Spirit.

So we have a request.
Today, this day,
> turn your face toward us.
Breathe your Spirit into our inert torpor, our slowness, our dormant selves,
> our wonderless efficiencies, our drained-out amazement,
and fill us with virulent energy,
> keenness in service, sharpness of wonderment,
> and willing spirit to pray, praise,
>> and sing of your blessed life-giving presence.

In the name of the Spirit-giver,

AMEN.

PSALM 29

Lord, our God,
>
>we stand to one side,
>
>while the heavenly beings practice their worship;

True to their calling they first praise you,
>
>attributing to you glory beyond compare,
>
>ascribing to you strength beyond measure,
>
>assigning to you the name of splendor.

From our tired lives, flattened from a week of weighty weariness,
>
>dulled from a barrage of incessant demands,
>
>dispirited by circumstances too heavy to bear,

— from our tired lives, gather us up in the worship of your heavens;
>
>call us, the deaf unhearing, into resounding worship;

drag us, the languid leaden, into dancing praise;
>
>beckon us, the sightless unconscious,
>
>>into enlightened thanksgiving,

that we may join all of heaven,
>
>and all who have gone before us,
>
>in devotion worthy of your holy splendor.

Now we hear your voice.

May your powerful voice
>
>speak against the demanding chaos of our week;

May your probing word
>
>establish the truly important in our week;

May your potent breath
>
>breathe new life into our dispirited week;

So that our shout of "Glory" may echo in our every hour,
>
>and this place of peace may underlie our every moment,
>
>and this time of blessing may mold all our conduct.

In the name of the powerful, blessed peacemaker,

AMEN.

PSALM 139:1–6, 13–18

It is you, Lord God, and it is I.
It is you, Lord God, and every I here today.

It is you and yours, and it is me, my, and mine.
It is you and yours, and it is every me, my, and mine here today.

It is you woven together with me, and every me in worship today.

A network, a plaiting, an intertwining of spirit, hope, intention;
    a fabric interwoven of your self, Lord God,
        and everyone connected in worship today.

Each thread of our conversation links with the matrix you have laid down
    from the beginning.
Each line of our communication has its origin
    in the first linking in the womb.
Each interlacing of souls traces its beginning
    to your first patterning.

How marvelous it is, Lord God,
    that you should intersect with us in such intimate ways.
You straighten even our knotted entanglements;
    you sort even our twisted enravelled lives;
    even our threadbare, matted relationships can discover new life.

For you, Lord God, are the great weaver, the re-knitter,
    the one who takes unruly skeins
        and forms, new, as yet unseen patterns,
    tying us into covenantal life with unbreaking cords.

Praise to you, Lord God,
    acquainted with all our ways,
    and loving us still.

AMEN.

PSALM 138

Lord God,
>   here in worship we encounter a transparent place,
>   where the veil between earth and heaven
>>   seems clear and crystalline.

Today we sing before the gods;
>   today we bow to the ground in this holy place.
In our worship we reach high
>   grasping your steadfast love and faithfulness;
in our worship we reach within
>   to call from our need and hopefulness.
Our souls are expanded;
our capacity for life and praise grows,
>   because today we mix it with the gods,
>   we join with the praise of kings and sovereigns;
and we hobnob with the lowly,
>   and ring out our gratitude with the humble meek.

For in this transparent place
>   where high and low meet in novel, new realm,
>   and where your name and word have unfettered freedom,
>   the old cramping bonds of class and pedigree,
>>   education and economics,
>>   suburb and profession,
>>   don't count.

And our souls are expanded,
>   no longer defensive of place and status,
>   freer to give and freer to receive,
>   ready to acknowledge your saving hand,
>   and be thankful.

For the hour,
>   your purpose is fulfilled
>   as we bathe in your steadfast love.

AMEN.

PSALM 20

The Sovereign, and the brothers and sisters of the Sovereign,
     appear before you this day, Lord God.

Into this court, royal or of justice,
     we voluntarily come.
Into this place of sacrifice and offering,
     this arena of vow-making and vow-taking,
     this assembly of witness-bearing and witness-forming,
     this congregation of celebration for new-born and dying,
into this place we firmly, solemnly, joyously
     declare your victory.

Any competing claim we reject from this hour;
any opposing force we deny power in this hour;
any other contender for sovereign status
     we will not recognize in this hour.

For our pride is in you alone, Lord our God —
     pride undiluted;
     pride uncompromised;
     pride without deviation.
Pride in you, your victory, your Godliness and lowliness
     your favor and forgivingness.
For you, the Lord, listen and answer when we call.

AMEN.

PSALM 9:9–20

Lord God, the drama is set to play.
The roles are defined, the stage ready, the theater in anticipation.
Except this drama is no play — it is real.
And the characters are not acting; the characters are us.
And the outcome, the resolution is not certain;
      the resolution is in jeopardy every day.
You, Lord God, chief playwright, director, and lead role,
     you, Lord, must rise up, for the drama is out of hand;
       evildoers contribute lines of merciless tragedy not in the script,
         and the needy are consigned to the wings.
Undirected, conniving strategists grab the limelight
     and the poor are not even stagehands.
Lord, when will you act in this dramatic epic?
When will you take charge of this farce of operatic proportions,
     controlled by an evil miscasting of players?
When will you make a scene change so that the poor and needy
     may escape from this enforced interlude and play a significant role?
Is it here, in this hour, that we should begin a new act?
Shall we here rehearse new lines, learn new songs, attend to new makeup?
For we can mask ourselves in powder and perfume, costume and grooming,
     but our inner life is somewhat shabby;
     and we need fresh reconciliations
        performing fresh forgivenesses.

Lord God, director in chief,
     look kindly on these amateurs and clothe us in forgiveness
     enough forgiveness to call forth honesty;
     enough pardon to provoke authentic sincerity;
     enough grace to stimulate truthfulness.
Break our reserve, our stage fright,
     our reluctant debut into the public scene,
so that freshly forgiven, pardoned and graced,
     we may have new lines to speak in the world's amphitheaters,
     and novel, never-before-performed theater to stage
        in the world's dramas
 — enough to make a difference
 — to your glory.

AMEN.

PSALM 130

Lord, our God,
        from the depths we cry.
Would you venture into the depths?
Would you, royally enthroned, allow yourself debasement,
        to hear one cry from the darkest place?

Why would you entertain empty purposelessness?
Would you recognize the voice of loneliness?
What do you know of secret abuse?
Is rape and violence a part of your repertoire?
Do you know of in-law wranglings
        and contorted marriage relationships?
Did your partner leave you — or did you have to leave?
Have you had grandchildren run wrong?
How has guilt wracked your conscience?
Where have soured business connections affected you?
When did your parent die?
Does grief tear at your insides?

These are our depths, Lord God;
        this is our darkness.

We cry the pathetic, painful, troubled cry of the damned,
        and we cannot stand tall, with integrity, without pretense.
Not yet; not yet.

So we wait; we wait until our plea penetrates your silence,
        and you act to companion our loneliness.
You, whose second name is steadfast love, redeemer, hope-giver.
We wait as those named after you.

In the name of One who has embraced the depths,

AMEN.

PSALM 48

Lord, our God,
> our congregation is not large,
> our building is not imposing,
> but we meet in the temple of the Most High!

Our people are ordinary people,
> our gathering is of regular individuals,
> but we gather with the daughters and sons of the Lord!

Our singing is habitual,
> and our music is familiar,
> but we raise music comparable with heaven's angels!

Our prayers are predictable,
> and our vernacular trite and commonplace,
> but we boldly converse with the great counsellor!

Our preaching drones in tedium,
> and our sermons, three-pointed, seldom prick,
> but we grapple with mighty, sharp, two-edged words!

Our shared peace-giving is perfunctory,
> and our benediction is a disguised period,
> but we invoke blessing from the original blessing-giver!

Lord God,
> who you are, who we are, and what we experience in this hour,
> are greater, more magnanimous, more fearfully astounding,
> and utterly forgiving than what we see.

We choose a holy place of your choosing, ordained by you,
> living by your hand,
> so beautifully wrought and safely gathered;

a heavenly host, lost in wonder, provoked to ponder,
reflecting on a foretaste of the city of God,
glad and rejoicing that you called and we came.

In the name of the One reaching the ends of the earth,

AMEN.

PSALM 24

Lord God
> as giver you have given a wonderful world,
> a well-ordered earth,
> a soil responsive to life-giving water,
> a sea producing food,
> weather patterns, growth and dying, summer and winter,
> all in fury and gentleness,
> beauty of blossom, and glowworm, and cold blue ice,
> fascinating bird song, and roar of beast,
>> and the silver thread of last night's snail.

Lord God, giver of life, creator of all,
> how can we respond out of gratitude
>> and genuine thankfulness?
How can we return obligation in proportion to gift rendered?

We will come to the place
> where praise is made and values shared;
we will stand in the presence of the holy,
> hands clean, hearts pure;
we will lift our souls to you, our God,
> and to no other.

Here we seek your blessing, your set rightness;
here we accompany your ordered gift of creation,
> with our faithful obedience — even more —
> your face we accompany with our heartfelt fearful praise.

So, enter, we plead! And may we enter, too,
> through these holy doors that witness
>> to the entry of a thousand saints.
Enter, we humbly ask, and may we enter, too, with you,
> powerful and glorious sovereign,
> strong and mighty,
> Lord of Lords gone before,
> God of creation and giver of Torah life.

In the name of the One who entered our lives,

AMEN.

PSALM 89:20–37

Lord God
> from the people he came;
> the sovereign one was born from among us.
Born from among us to rule on earth as you rule in heaven.
Lord, for your part you make promise, vow, and oath
> to your chosen one.
> For our part...?
Lord, for your part you pledge steadfast love and faithfulness.
> For our part...?
Lord, for your part you make solemn covenant
> never to be broken.
> For our part...?
For if we are to do your will on earth as it is done in heaven,
> we must respond,
> chosen as we are, aligning ourselves with the chosen One.
So we cry out, "Father, God, Rock of Salvation; hear us!"
For our part, we give up on your guidance,
> we violate your ways,
> we don't keep your commandments.

Your promise, vow, oath, pledge, and covenant
> don't meet their match in us;
> we are not reciprocating;
> the binding is not mutual, and we know it.
Your will done in heaven is not done on earth.
Lord, our God, for our part, we would turn again,
> and renew our part.
We say the vow again:
> "We will follow you our whole life long.
> We will follow you our whole life long."
As you don't lie to us
> nor will we lie to you.
As you are true to us,
> we will be true to you.
So may your will be done on earth as it is in heaven.

AMEN.

PSALM 14

Who rules the world, Lord God?
Because we are here, we are inclined to say you rule.

But we notice, as you notice,
    some are bent on impossible autonomy.
They never quite articulate their atheism,
    but they live it.
We know, and you know,
    because of the world's endless corruption reported to us.
Who rules the world, Lord God?
We want desperately to say you rule.

But we observe, as you observe,
    poor without bread, and helpless without protection,
    caused by those who set rules without reference to you.
We know it, and you know it,
    because of starvation reported to us.
Who rules the world, Lord God?
We are committed to saying you rule.

But we heed, as you heed,
    the bulletins of family violence and sexual abuse,
    and relationships of brutality,
    caused by those who have no clue
        of your rule of neighbor care.
We know it, and you know it,
    because abuse is so rife in your world.
Lord, we still assert you are the ruler;
    you rule from heaven and side with the poor
    even in the world skewed by fools.
And as the baptized, signed-on members of your task force,
    we submit to your rule,
    and we perpetuate your government.
You have our vote.

In the name of the One who cast his vote for us,

AMEN.

PSALM 51:1–12

Seldom do we come to such admissions, Lord God;
seldom do we acknowledge our sin-induced forsakenness;
seldom do we accept our wrongs have jeopardized,
     violated our relating to you,
     and have plunged us into grim, horrifying loneliness.
We seek to compensate our loneliness,
     pretending things are different;
     diversionary texts learnt in the marketplace
        occupy our meager hopefulness,
     but none address our inner poverty.
That is all we have to offer here in worship,
     O God — nothing in hand,
     but a clinging across the void to your offered mercy.
Yes, we have sinned,
yes, we have mutinied,
yes, we have usurped your agenda
     and countered with contaminating texts of our own,
     texts we act on, which injure others and violate you.
O God, into our dulled, soggy minds hammer home the texts of healing;
     blot out transgression, wash me, cleanse me,
     purge me, create in me a clean heart,
     put a new spirit in me, restore new joy of salvation,
     sustain me.
Form for us the new context for our lives,
     for only you can,
     from your mercy, your steadfast love, your abundant mercy.
And then we will be grateful,
     abundantly grateful,
     in your presence, O God;
     sin hidden and crushed,
     newly spirited, with joy and gladness;
     truth-seekers, wisdom-learners.
Thanks be to you, O God.
Who can condemn us?
Only Jesus Christ.
In the name of Jesus Christ
     we are forgiven.

AMEN.

PSALM 130

Lord God, have you heard our saying,
      "It's not what you know, but who you know?"
We come into worship this day seeking you, the one whom we know.

For our world is beautiful but dangerous
      and the danger overwhelms us;
sin sucks us down into its vortex;
pollutants and wastes left from humanity's self-will
      contaminate all our space;
wrong perpetuated floods our struggling lives.

We know it, but it's not what we know,
      it's who we know that counts.

Out of the depths we cry:
Hear us! Attend to us! See us!

Should you watch us as one marking down our contributions to
polluted life,
      we have no chance. We drown.

But you are not like that;
you are a forgiver, not a moral accountant,
      a pardoner, not an ethical checkout god,
      a pass-over God, not a police god.

You are the "who" we know,
      who second-rates all the "whats" we know.
For it is not what we know, but who we know
      that draws us into forgiven communion.

So we wait patiently, urgently, expectantly;
      we watch persistently, hopefully, contentedly,
         for you, Lord God,
         powerful redeemer, steadfast lover,
         whom we know.

AMEN.

PSALM 111

Lord, our God,
>
> into the patterned worship of this day
> we regulate our undisciplined, intermittent flights
> > of private devotion,
>
> we order here, our irregular piety within your ordered life,
> we arrange our muddled prayer probes into proper sequence.

For you, Lord God,
perpetuate an ordered creation circumscribed by covenant
 — a creation holding firmly together
 — a creation sustained by trust and promise.
So we come confidently, seeking life's blessed coherence
> within coherent covenantal communion today.

In the company of the congregation
> we thank you wholeheartedly.

We recognize your handiwork in the earth;
we perceive your commitment to our unfolding history;
we acknowledge your hand in our social interactions;
we thank you for our life and health and daily food.

We notice, as you notice,
> that rightness brings its blessing
> and crookedness cripples all it touches.

We notice, as you notice,
> that generosity shares its beneficial influence,
> and greed grinds mischief into raw wrong.

We notice, as you notice,
> that commitment to the worshiping community
> provides stability in unstable, floundering community life.

Lord God, may our wisdom in your covenantal world increase,
> may our wisdom of your covenantal intentions appreciate,
> as we practice our fearfully wonderful liaison with you.

Holy and awesome is your name among us.

AMEN.

PSALM 84

How we would love to find the precise place you live, Lord God.
How we would love to discover the real center of life,
    the perfect number,
    the final resolution,
    the definitive answer to every complex question.
How we would love to quit our searching
    and arrive at pure truth,
    explain every complexity,
    resolve every conundrum.

But you don't live in a world of sterile answers,
    because sterile answers lead to misused power
        and diminishing hope.

You deal in trusting conversations,
    places of communion,
    environments of joyful discourse.
Your commodities are in safe havens,
    places of delight,
    sanctuaries for robust, peaceful rest.

How we would love to nurture your presence,
    even get a foot on the threshold of your residence
    even for a moment.

How we would love to cultivate your companionship,
    even for a shadow of your favor,
    even for an hour of holy honor.

How we would love to imbibe your spirit,
    even a taste, even a sweet sip.

Lord of hosts, spare one of your emissaries
    to demonstrate the life of love, relationship, and sacrifice.

In the name of the One spared for resurrection,

AMEN.

PSALM 45:1–2, 6–9

We gather in public worship, our God,
    because we have life themes too great
        to squander in private devotion
    and texts worthy of kingly scrutiny.
We have something to say.

Clothed in God-given grace
    we come before you as handsome praise-makers.
Wearing God-given garments of righteousness
    we flourish our blessings, named one by one.
Covered in a cloak of forgiveness
    our usually over-talkative, excuse-laden mouths
    pour forth the murmur of contented well-being.

Because for the moment, in the hour,
    we choose to live in the coming kingdom
        of your creative inclusion,
    and not the decaying earthliness of our bungled making.

So hear us, our God,
    blessed as we are with daughters, sons, friends,
    laughter, companionship, partners,
    parents, peers, sister, brother;
hear us recount our blessings and lodge them
    in your eternal memory so we may revisit them;
listen to our joyful freedoms of this moment and deposit them
    in your treasury so we may wear them in the safe times;
join us in displaying the good news fashion lines of grace,
    righteousness, and forgiveness,
    that we may dare to wear them in the street,
    and smell your sweet gladness in our wake.

For your home, your demeanor, your holy accents,
    we want to perpetuate
    for your glory and the world's salvation.

AMEN.

PSALM 125

Lord, our God,
>   our world is full of ambiguities and enigmas.
Why does wickedness have its destructive way?
Why does evil weigh in so heavy?
How does the demonic move so stealthily
>   to surface in unexpected places,
>   even in our own hearts?

Lord our God,
>   we admit to our dependence on you,
>   for we have tried the independence route
>   >   and it dead-ends in grief.
We cannot occupy the center place;
we don't have the capacity to sustain autonomy;
we can only gather around the holy place,
>   and then be gathered around by you, the Holy God.

Surround us, we pray,
>   that we might not be destroyed by wickedness,
>   that we might not be weighed heavy by evil,
>   that the stealthy demonic may find no congenial resting place.

And then surround us, we pray,
>   that we might find the path of goodness through life's ambiguities,
>   that we may still trust you in spite of life's enigmas,
>   that we might learn well-doing and doing well.

We place trust in you for this hour.
May we learn trust in the hour when not a lot is at stake,
>   so that in the marketplace, where a lot is at stake,
>   we will still trust you
>   and so remain with you.

In the name of One who elected rightness and rejected crooked ways,

AMEN.

PSALM 19

Lord God, we are ready to enjoy your creation.
We marvel at its radiant beauty,
>we are surprised by its hidden intricacies,
>we are dazzled by its magnificent brilliance,
>and we respect its wild fury and power.

Lord God, we are ready to consider your Torah instruction.
We wonder at its broad comprehensiveness,
>we are perplexed at its deceptive simplicity,
>we are fascinated by its endless invitation to conversation,
>and we are astonished at its knowingness.

Lord God,
>your word that brought forth creation,
>also brought forth your Torah law,
>>a guidance we might follow.
But our difficulty with both is a rampant self.
We have problems with our drive for self-centering autonomy,
>our urge for a fashionable self-assertion,
>our pressured inducements for self-advancement.
So we threaten your creation and we bend your Torah word.

Lord God,
>we are ready at least in this hour,
>to produce Torah compliance,
>and to entertain respect for creation.
For our souls need reviving,
>battered as they are by a callous self;
we seek wisdom to keep self in trim;
we welcome a rejoicing heart and enlightened eyes,
>enabling us to enjoy one's self-giving self.
Our meditations, our word,
>may they find your acceptance;
>for, Lord God, we are ready for a redeemed self,
>>an amazed self, an obedient selflessness.

In the name of the selfless servant king,

AMEN.

PSALM 1

Lord God, you set stark choices before us today.
You ask of us unequivocal decision making.
You deal out an alternative and withhold options.
> And we are uneasy.

Because we like ambiguity — it avoids choosing;
> we love a plethora of options — we can dither forever;
> we favor complexity — we can plead ignorance,
> > or argue interminably, or both.
But here you place before us clear choice:
> wickedness or righteousness,
> lost misery or knowing delight,
> perishing neglect or persisting stance,
> blown chaff or yielding fruitfulness,
> forgotten disappearedness or nourished plentyness.

And we are uneasy.
Is there no neutral place?
Is there no center to consider possibilities?
Is there no bargaining or negotiation?
It seems not.
You have laid it out before us; either way we will confront limits.
And it is not easy.

But enough trouble has come our way to provoke a rethink.
We are familiar with wickedness, lost misery,
> perishing neglect, blown chaff.
We seek righteousness, knowing delight,
> persisting stance, yielding fruitfulness.
For this way is delight beyond measure, for you and for us.
Push us, heave us, lever us, lead us,
> into the place of obedient submission,
> and for your and our sakes,
> save us from all other options.

In the name of the One who made the choice,

AMEN.

PSALM 124

Lord, our God,
     Israel is not alone in enduring enemy attack.
We, too, come under siege, assaulted, invaded.

It's our rage, carefully controlled and stuffed out of sight.
It's our despair, masked by a smile.
It's our waning trust, buried by a loud song.
It's our fear, denied in our busy service.
It's our pain, set aside for the next affirmation of faith.
Each attack corrodes our formerly strong supports,
        and collapse seems imminent unless you intervene on our side,
           Lord God.

Give us permission to re-examine our former believing selves;
Give us leave to re-assess faith formed in a previous life;
Give us the warrant to search for a more adequate trust base.
Because if you don't
        we will be swallowed whole, swept away, overwhelmed,
        our community will break up and break down,
        our neighborliness will disintegrate,
        our honesty and integrity will crumble.
So Lord God,
        it is a big ask, a risky move;
        but because you are faithfully tenacious,
        for us and not against us,
        we would fly as a bird from a prison,
        escape from the inadequate faith
           that once held but now doesn't.

And we trust you to search with us
     for the new landing place.
Our help is in the name of the Lord
     who made heaven and earth.

AMEN.

PSALM 26

Lord God, we are here;
we are in the place of well-loved public worship,
    the place where saints have worshiped,
because here your glory has focus,
    and our devotion converges in concerted adoration.

Lord God, we admit to our stupid sinfulness,
    our willful sidestep to doing justice and making peace.
But we want you to hear of other matters today.

We have been walked on.
We have suffered through others' vindictiveness.
Abuse has assaulted us;
    victims we are of those more powerful,
    battered by unbidden forces not of our determining.
And we speak for thousands snared in someone else's battle.

Worse, Lord God.
We are seduced by evil.
We are tempted to take on the tactics of our attackers.
We are capable of hypocrisy and wickedness, of evil and bribery.

But God, we cry out to you on two fronts:
  — don't let us share in the bloodthirsty strategies of the aggressors,
    and vindicate us in our faithfulness, our integrity, our trust;
  — prevent us from taking on the mantle of the assailants,
    and in your judgment, acquit us of any wrong shadowing us.

So now, in this place of well-loved worship,
    a great congregation where saints have leveled with you before,
    where your glory dwells and our devotion gathers,
we sing, we commune, we walk in integrity,
    trusting and testing, joyful and judged,
    playful and proven, vindicated.

In the name of the suffering One, vindicated,

AMEN.

PSALM 22:1–15

Lord, our God,
>you are the holy one, but you forgot us;
>you, the praised one, but you forsook us;
>you, the trusted one, but you close your ears on us.

Why?

Our forebears trusted you and you saved them;
>they cried to you and you intervened.

Why do you shame us?
How come you cause loss of face when you promise so much,
>and deliver so little?
Your saving power is reduced to a whimper.
Even in public broadcasting and private conversation
>we are cynically taunted,
>>because you have not done what you said you would do.

We remember your motherly protection,
we recall your maternal nurture,
>and now you drop us from memory.
Not one of your children's cries penetrates the curtain on heaven.
Why?

So in your distant silence,
>we wear roaring scorn,
>>ravenous disparagement, screeching mockery;
and we are reduced to shriveled silence,
>melting, evaporating into nothingness.
With our last cry we rasp out our desperate hope;
>for we are deeply troubled, and no one else can help.
Save us, our God! Save us.
Look beyond our facade of proud competency.
Look beneath the mask of polite civility.
Discover our wretchedness,
>and answer us with words to save.

In the name of word made flesh,

AMEN.

PSALM 104:1–9, 24, 35c

From our one small point in the universe,
    we contemplate your greatness, O God.
From the half square foot we occupy on earth,
    we marvel at your well-created playground.
A blaze of light from sun, moon, star,
        cloud filtered in glorious array,
        settles on our tiny retina,
        and we are amazed!
A dome of blue punctuated by ever-changing cumulus, nimbus, cirrus
        seasons our weather,
        and our garden grows — common awesomeness!
A wind of balmy breeze to force ten,
        breath to blast, whiff to whirlwind,
        fans our small acre,
        and we live — astounding gentleness!
The ever-evolving earth quakes and grinds,
        erodes and silts, in changing permanence
        and we ride a foot of topsoil — astonishing precariousness!
The water of the earth rains and vapors,
        snows and melts, falls to common level,
        flood tide and ebb,
        with boundaries fixed in minor variation,
        and fish on Friday — delicate balance!

From our one small point,
from our half square foot we stand agog;
        we wonder at your wisdom,
        confounded by your countless creatures.
Thank you for our half square foot,
        this sure place to stand,
        this piece of holy ground.
We are grateful our small piece of place
        is honored by you, great God.
Bless the Lord, O my soul.
Praise the Lord.

AMEN.

PSALM 34:1–8

Lord, our God,
>we grasp the opportunity to intercede for the dispossessed.

As we worship here in the company of confidence,
>we pray for the humble dispirited,
>that they may find gladness.

As we occupy a place of safety,
>we pray for those beset by fearfulness,
>that they may find reassuring word and a way out of despair.

As we take up our familiar place of honor in your house,
>we pray for those disgraced in shame,
>that they may discover dignity and reinstated reputation.

We give thanks for the riches that adorn our selves and homes;
>we pray for poverty-stricken homeless refugees,
>crying to be heard,
>that they may find salvation out of trouble.

With the accouterments of confidence, safety, honor, and riches,
we join with the humble dispirited,
>the fearful beset,
>the shameful disgraced,
>the poverty-stricken,

that we all may taste and see your goodness, Lord,
that we all may discover the place of happy refuge,
that we all may find reflected radiance before you,
that we all may hear your word due to us.

So may we — the confident, safe, honored, rich
>and them — the humbled, fearful, shamed, poor —
together magnify you, Lord,
and exalt your name together.

And, perchance, we may be provoked to move toward equity.

In the name of the humble poor One,

AMEN.

PSALM 146

We praise you in this place of worship, Lord God;
    we sing and say, call and pray in this odd liturgy.
For we know the liturgy of commerce and contract,
    combat and contest, competition and conflict.
We know they are all found wanting;
    they do not deserve our absolute trust,
    because they run dry of generative life;
    they die, helpless, perishing.
But here we practice alternative liturgy,
    liturgy conceived in your mind, Lord God,
    and born at the moment of creation.
"Let there be…and it was so" is the creative word that informs our liturgy.
"I will never again destroy…" is the reassuring word
    that signifies our liturgy.
"I will make covenant with…" is the powerful word that shapes our liturgy.
Lord God, in this hour
    our practices are different, our perspectives distinct,
        our possibilities boundless,
    because in covenantal communion
        we share in a different worldview;
    a view shaped by exodus and promise,
        by exile and restoration,
        by crucifixion and resurrection,
        by Godly rule and Godly peace.

So our prayers are bold because writ large is the backdrop:
    "Is anything too hard for the Lord?"
Prisoners, Lord — set bound-up people free.
Blind ones, Lord — set the darkened unseeing free.
Bowed-down ones, Lord — straighten up for freedom.
Strangers, orphans, widows, all sidelined ones, Lord —
    free at last in the place of honor.
For in our liturgy,
    you reign, and we entertain for the moment a free, just world.

In the name of One who proclaimed freedom and justice,

AMEN.

PSALM 127

Lord God,
>we anxious ones gather,
>fatigued before the week begins,
>rising early, bedding late,
>because we believe our labor, our toil, our nervous watching,
>motivated by failure fear, will build the home we want;

but the toll is alarming, and we need to hear a new word.
We punctuate our drive, our ambition, our goal achieving,
>with vow-taking, love-making, home-building,
>child-rearing, mortgage-paying, building the home we want;

but the demands are perilous, and we need to hear a new word.
For our hard work may satisfy our customers,
>and kill us;

and our best intentions may build the shell of companionable life,
>and kill our families.

And sometimes our best work dissipates in frustrated disappointment,
>or no work at all;

and our hopeful vow-taking twists to regretful vow-breaking,
>or no vow at all.

We need to hear, we urgently need to hear, a new word;
>words which say, blessedness and received restedness,
>giftedness and enjoyed fruitfulness,
>yieldedness and delight in rewardedness.

For on Sabbath day
>we admit we are not the center of human endeavor.

You are, Lord God, and we are learning to trust you.
Break in on our lonely ambitions,
>our vocations and family,
>with new words of yielding, rewardedness;
>gifting, fruitfulness; blessing, restedness;

a trusting that you will provide as you said you would
>even for us, for me.

In the name of the One who lived trust,

AMEN.

PSALM 16

Lord God,
  we come to Sabbath worship
    to replenish our meager trust reserves,
  and cultivate our trust capabilities.

We come in company with those who put their trust in you
   those who discover trusting bears fruitfulness,
   those who discover affairs with other gods deplete
    the capacity to trust.

We come within the story of those whose blessing correlates
  with their trusting
  those who dodge hell by glad trust in you.

We come using the peculiar vocabulary of daring trusters
  those whose common talk is,
    "pleasant places," "goodly heritage,"
    "fullness of joy," "pleasures evermore,"
  those whose speech reflects your power and our security.

We come within the counterculture of focused trusters
  those whose first choice is Godly portion,
  those who learn trust with you and risk trusting others.

We come to walk the uncommon trust path,
  in company,
  within the story,
  with a peculiar vocabulary,
  within a counterculture.

In the name of One who trusted self to you and us,

AMEN.

PSALM 132:1–12

Lord God,
we rouse ourselves above, beyond, our limited intellect,
 our confined wisdom,
 our bounded capacities.
We come into your chosen space with your chosen people,
 to meet your chosen sovereign One;
and perchance our boundaries, our confinements,
 our limits may expand,
and our capacities, our wisdom, our intellect, may increase.

For the hour,
 we occupy the same space,
 we cohabit the same home,
 we rest in the same place as you, Lord God;
For the hour,
 the righteousness you wear, we wear,
 the language you employ, we employ,
 the vows you make, we make.
For the hour,
 your memory is our memory,
 your intentions are our intentions,
 your hopes are our hopes.

So Lord God,
 rouse yourself!
Sovereign God,
 bring your glory, for we are here.
Remembering God,
 honor your covenant in this, your resting place,
 that your chosen One may engage our intellect,
  our wisdom, our capacities,
 and sins forgiven,
 and freedoms begun,
 and loving rampant.

In the name of the chosen sovereign,

AMEN.

Year C

THE YEAR
OF LUKE

PSALM 25:1–10

Indeed it is to you, Lord God, that we lift souls.
It is for you we wait — in you we put our trust.

And while we struggle with our humility, or lack of it,
     on this occasion of worship
     we honestly seek your way for us
        — open to your paths
        — listening for your truth
        — acknowledging you, the center of life.

Because here we acknowledge that in the end we cannot manage
     our own lives
        — that some things are out of our control
        — that life is too vast and complex for us to understand all that is.
Help us to be open to mystery, your mystery among us,
     your mysterious presence that calms us,
        and holds us in every circumstance.

We are grateful for your well-developed memory
        — remembering us, who we are,
           your well-loved creatures
        — and remembering us,
           motivated by your steadfast love and mercy for us.
And we are grateful for your well-developed ability to forget
        — forgetting our shameful acts
        — our dubious behavior
        — our foolishness of youth and age.
For you do not hold the past against us
        — but you give us reason and confidence to begin again,
        — freed of a guilt
        — lightened of a burden
        — loved and able to love.

God of grace
     help us to claim fruitful, full future,
     partnering you in good life, forgiven life, full life, wholesome life.

In the name of Jesus Christ, our stand-in before you,

AMEN.

PSALM 27

A strong, fearless psalm, O God
      — a thumbing of noses at evil adversaries,
      — a courageous, confident stand against all that would destroy,
      — because we spend time in residence in the Lord's home:
            — learning the tricks of survival
            — what snags and what liberates
            — what exposes to danger and what protects
            — what lays us low and what lifts us high.
But our experience falls short of our best hopes.

We have one eye on your light
      and the other on seductive neons.
We have one foot in your stronghold
      and the other in shifting sands.
We are often in cohoots with the enemy
      — sabotaging our ethical norms
      — diluting our intellectual integrity
      — declassifying our precious mysteries
      — divulging confidences shared
      — pirating our moral stances
      — compromising our best selves.

No wonder we cry aloud:
      "Be gracious to us! Hear us!
      Do not turn away in anger!
      Do not cast us off!
      Do not forsake us!"

Our hearts cry out to remind us — insist — that we seek your face, O Lord;
      but our imprudent selves bribe us into slippery action,
      unbecoming of a member of your household.
So teach us, and teach us, and teach us.
May we wait, and wait, and wait
      so we see your goodness, O Lord.

In the name of the One for whom we wait,

AMEN.

PSALM 45

As we place ourselves in worship,
> as we divest ourselves of the frenzy of pre-Christmas,
> and engage ourselves with the goodly theme of the year,
> our tongues like pens writing our praise through the liturgy,
> transcribing our acclaim into spoken word,
> composing with vague scribblings
>> and artistic calligraphy our chorus and canticle,
> songs to the praise of our God.

Your brilliance attracts us;
> your splendor captivates us;
> your grace delights us;
> your power astonishes us.

You defend truths we thought indefensible;
> you teach realities we calculated unimaginable;
> you defeat enemies we believed insurmountable.

Your home endures years, nations, cultures, ages;
> your justice pursues persistent wrong;
> your righteousness outlives warped wickedness.

Honor and reverence are due to you
> the best of fragrant perfume
> the finest of robes
> the masterpiece of music.

We come as residents within the Lord's household
> defending new truth
> imagining new possibilities
> defeating old enemies
> revelling in the new home
> upholding new levels of justice
> fighting entrenched wickedness
> matching our new surroundings with the best we can offer
> as perfect, faultless, and spotless as we are able for the hour;
> celebrating, boasting, praising, bragging, triumphing
>> in our adopted home.
> To the absolute glory of God.

In the name of the glorious Child to come,

AMEN.

PSALM 80:1–7

Restore us, O Lord God,
    let your face shine, that we might be saved.

May our homes receive the gift of your healing grace
    that binds up the wounds we so carelessly inflict on each other.

May our congregation receive the gift of compassionate understanding,
    that we may increase in appreciation of each other's differences
    and recognize ourselves truly as sisters and brothers.

May our community receive the gifts
        of wise leadership and courageous citizenship,
    that people of goodwill might make this community more
        humane,
    more caring, more concerned about the vulnerable.

May our nation receive the gifts
        of greater tolerance, and broader vision;
    may we truly know and appreciate that we need each other.

May the nations of the world receive the gift of new possibilities
    for a sane and decent future together,
    an end to the madness
        of centuries-old alienation and hatred between peoples;
    may you protect the nations' peoples
        in perilous times of change and disruption.

May we all receive, O God, the gift of joy and peace,
    and a powerful sense of welcoming
        as we anticipate in this Advent season,
    some of the ways in which the spirit of your Beloved Child
        comes into our lives,
            our church,
            our world.

We pray in the name of the coming One,

AMEN.

Since the Lectionary suggests the same psalms for Year C as in Years A and B, please refer to the Christmas prayers for those earlier years.

PSALM 29

The universe is your arena, O God.
The world is your opera house.
The whole of nature is your theater.
The earth's acoustics well reflect your glory.
The accents are clear, the intonations compelling, the word articulate.

When we hear your kind of oratory,
when your rhetoric strikes a chord, and your speech registers,
        then we draw strength for our living.

For who can quiet the thunderer?
Who can make impotent the powerful One?
Who can dethrone the majestic One?

We say, "None!"
So we will stand against all who stand against you
        for the world's peace.
We will support justice between the nations
        for the world's peace.
We will repulse misused power in families and communities
        for the world's peace.

Then Godly-motivated peace will bless all nations,
        and all peoples will gladly volunteer for submissive obedience
            to your holy regenerative will.

May the Lord bless God's people with peace.

AMEN.

PSALM 36:5–10

Lord God,
        may your steadfast love
        come to this congregation of your people today
        — your steady, strong, sustaining love —
        may we know it today as we await your Spirit.

Lord God,
        we come with clouded minds and troubled spirits
        struggling for survival,
        often in argument with someone,
        often enduring long-term confrontation with people close to us,
        often preferring to avoid people
                because of fracture and awkwardness between us.

Left to ourselves, we seem to perpetuate the fractures.

But you, Lord God, promise to intervene
        — the third untainted party —
        to bring light and life to our awkward relationships.

It is indeed in your light
        that we see light.
It is the drink you give
        that soothes the harsh rasp in our voice.
It is the feasting you provide
        that satisfies our inner hunger.

Lord, our God, today
        come once more
        come anew
        come afresh
that we each may know the warm glow of Spirit,
        and endure the searing burn of conviction,
        and rejoice in the purifying flame of past forgiven.

Through Christ our Lord,

AMEN.

PSALM 19

We do not presume to come into your presence as if by right,
Lord God
        — we come on your invitation only.

So may our thinking,
      our speaking,
      our meditation
          be acceptable to you, the Holy God.

As we view your creation, and contemplate your world around us,
      we see signs of creation's praise,
      a praise that emerges unsummoned,
          never waiting to be acknowledged
          but simply arraying the world with exquisite beauty.

We, too, wish to commune with creation,
      but when we lose its intention of bringing glory to you,
          the Creator,
      it falls flat, its life is gone; it is so fleeting.
Your creation, without your glory, makes no demand,
      offers no lasting relationship,
      and lulls us into soulless slumber;
      enjoyable, but lacking rewarding depth.

So, Lord God, immerse us in your creation that reflects your glory,
      and may the words of our mouths,
      and the meditations of our hearts,
          be acceptable to you,
          our Lord, our Rock, our Redeemer.

AMEN.

PSALM 71:1–6

Lord God, hear our prayer.

Our lives digest a desperate menu daily dished,
      a pottage of refuge and shame,
      righteousness and wickedness,
      rescue and injustice.

Our community hunger for violence alarms us;
our appetite for cruelty intimidates us;
our bulimic grasping appalls us.

We imagine the sustaining safety of the womb,
      deeply compassionate, secure, protective.

But we are thrust into a world of ravenous predators
      — older, stronger, shrewder.
And our overfed minds,
      pickled and preserved by a diet
          of a media dedicated to brutality,
      easily become paranoid and fearful.

Lord God, hear our prayer,
      and feed us an alternative diet,
a diet of unashamedness in your presence,
a nurturing in your righteousness,
sustenance in your salvation,
a provision of trust and hope.

May communion within the strong fortress
      be our daily bread.

In the name of the One who hears prayers,

AMEN.

PSALM 138

I give you thanks, O Lord, with my whole heart.

Lord, set your blessing on us, as we begin this day together.
With gratitude of heart, we come into your holy presence,
> to love and be loved, to give and to receive,
> to be forgiven and to forgive.
Confirm in us the truth by which we rightly live.
Confront in us the truth from which we wrongly turn.

All the kings of the earth shall praise you, O Lord.

From Africa, may your hear the praise of rulers and people.
From the Middle East, may you hear the praise
> of Jew and Palestinian.
From the Americas, may you hear the praise
> of presidents, of immigrants, of indigenous peoples.
From Europe, may you hear the praise of premiers and peasants,
> and on this day — from victims, victors and vanquished.
From Asia, may you hear the praise of witnesses to your truth.
From Australia, may you hear the praise
> of Pakeha, Maori, Aborigine.

Though I walk in the midst of trouble, you preserve me.

Lord, in the times when we feel we are losing hope,
> or feel our efforts are futile,
let us see in our hearts and minds
> the image of your resurrection;
let that be the source of our courage and strength.

With that, and in your company,
> help us to face challenges and struggles
> against all that hurts us,
> and against all that is born of inhumanness and injustice.

The Lord will fulfill his purpose for us.
Your steadfast love, O Lord, endures forever.

Thanks be to God.

AMEN.

PSALM 1

Choices, choices, Lord God.
Stark choices.
Clear, unavoidable choices.
Choices we make early in life,
        which bear directly on later life.
Choices between happiness, blessedness,
        and bitterness, wickedness.

But God, we learn too late of your law
        and too early of our repugnant self-will.

Would you entertain latecomers?
Would you permit into your congregation slow learners?
Would you let loose your liturgy of love on the lapsed loyal?

Now we are here in public worship,
        introduce us, we pray, to your law
        — to give ballast to our souls —
            and keep us upright;
        and show us how to jettison bilge rubbish
        — which carries no weight —
            and is driven away by the wind.

Then we may follow the advice of the heaven-born,
        and take the path the blessed tread,
        and sit in the seat of benediction,
                bearing the fruit of the season,
                offering shade to the beaten,
                always tenderly watched over by you,
                    the righteous, fearsome, choice-offering
                    God.

AMEN.

PSALM 37:1–11, 39–40

God, you make things sound so frustratingly easy!
Do you expect us to give up our fretfulness
    without a murmur?
Do you expect us to put our envy quietly away
    without raised voice of indignation?
Do you expect us to quash our anger
    at the evil prosperous?
Don't you know our honest toil
    for scant reward?
Don't you know our little recompense
    for loyal hard work?
Don't you know our lack of recognition
    for years of dedication?

We do fret!
    We are envious!
        We are angry!

So, is this word today for people like us?
It is difficult for us to trust you alone,
    in the face of widespread dubious gain.
It is hard on our commitment levels
    in a crass consumer environment.
Our patience is sorely tested
    amidst the parade of the opulent.

But we plead;
    would you save us from fretful decay,
        and pollutant envy, and contaminating anger.
And would you claim our attention,
    delight our hearts, and instill a patient waiting;
so that contentment pervades our souls,
    and trust in your providential care
        tingles our minds.

In the name of One sowing seeds of hope among us,

AMEN.

PSALM 92:1–4, 12–15

We thank you, Lord God,
>   for diverting our attention away from ourselves
>   for levering our self-consciousness sideways
>   for winding our wearied selves from center place.

We thank you, Lord God,
>   that there is another listener in our world
>   that there is another speaker in the conversation
>   that there is another counsel to follow.

We thank you, Lord God,
>   that we can make fresh declarations of ready love
>   that we note alternative language of music
>   that gratitude is a counterplot in life.

We thank you, Lord God,
>   that our times are a window for fresh insight
>   that mornings offer the vision of steady love
>   that evenings present a view of daily faithfulness.

May our other-generated gladness
>   cause us to sing for joy,
>   and thus nourish our inner selves
>   and produce unbounded contentment.

So, with our roots in your house,
>   our language will be a fanfare of praise,
>   from the youngest to the oldest,
>   to your glory.

AMEN.

PSALM 99

Lord God, the announcement is made: "The Lord is King!"
 Who holds the power? It is not us!
We hear the announcement as comfort and rebuke;
comfort in that in our moments of weakness and vulnerability,
 you are the one who has the power to care;
comfort in that when humanity's power runs rampant,
 in the end your power will hold sway.
And rebuke;
 rebuke in that we cannot claim too much;
 we cannot promise what we cannot give;
 we cannot control too much.

So the announcement is made: "The Lord is King!"
 Who holds the power? It is not us!
We are grateful that you, the powerful one,
 are a lover of justice,
and that is sometimes too much for us to bear
 because we aren't lovers of justice;
 we merely like justice when it is for us.
And you are one who establishes equity,
 and that is sometimes too much for us to bear
 because fairness is demanding,
 and righteousness is blindingly bright
  when we care for a little dark inequity in our favor.

Yet you love us still,
nudging us, urging us, carrying us,
nurturing us, lifting us,
 giving us a new place to stand,
 a new way to live,
 a fresh sighting of the world.
God of justice, equity, righteousness,
 at least for this hour you are our Lord, our God.

Praise to you, O Holy God,
 through Christ our Lord,
AMEN.

PSALM 91:1–2, 9–16

Lord, our God,
not often do we hear your direct speech to us,
but here you speak:
> "Those who love me, I will deliver;
I will protect those who know my name.
When they call to me, I will answer them;
I will be with them in trouble,
I will rescue them and honor them.
With long life I will satisfy them,
and show them my salvation."

That is what we hoped for;
that is how we understand your promise,
> mediated by your priests and ministers.
Now we hear it, your own speech in our own ears.

As we venture out of safe cocoons,
> into unpredictable, risky, dangerous journey,
> may our earthly encounters
> find an underpinning truth in your word.
May the fearless claims from heaven
> match the fearful contingencies of earth.

And may we face the threats God-following adventurers experience
> with a confidence pinned on you, God,
> the Most High, the Almighty,
> the One in whom we trust.

AMEN.

PSALM 27

Lord, our God,
we wait and we hope,
we gather strength and we take courage.

For we have discovered the center of life is in worship,
      living in the home of the living,
        resting in grace-giving sacramental space,
        learning from value-laden tradition.

From the center,
      we will face all that evil will throw at us.
We will face vicious and persistent annoyance
      and we will stand firm
      because our center remains still in worship.
We will face lawful injustice and lawless violation,
      and we will stand firm
      because our still center remains in worship.

Lord, our God,
      meet us at the center
      because without you
          the center becomes as dreadful as the brutal edges.

Teach us, love us, instruct us, shame us
      into faithful living and gospel behavior;
      because our center must be different from
         the corrupt world we live in;
      at center we must not copy the pollution of our environment.

At center is our hope of fresh new patterns for living.

So overwhelm us with strong goodness, we pray.

To your glory,

AMEN.

PSALM 63:1–8

Lord God,
>   are you really water-bearer for the parched thirsty?
>   Will you really uplift a tired, flagging body?

Because as we live out our lives in your world,
>   as we seek to act as Christ's body in our community,
>   we become wrung out, dry, needing refreshment.

We need to know of your refreshing strength,
>   to recognize it and claim it;
>   because our strength is taken, leached out,
>   · in battling injustices in your world.

We seek a community where all races are respected
>   and receive their just rights.
We work for a community where people — children, men, women —
>   are freed from exploitation powered by others.
We want a community where all know they are loved and belong.
And in the battle, we become tired, wilted.
So we come to the sanctuary
>   to drink in your glory and love,
>   that cracked lips may praise you
>   and raw throat may sing hearty thanksgiving.

For our lives are restored by a steadfast love, greater than life,
>   and in the place of worship, shaded on the lee-side of your table,
>   feasted on your sacramental presence,
>   we may go in fruitful resolve,
>   as your agent in the world modeling Christ's life in our community.

In the name of the Cross-bearer,

AMEN.

PSALM 32

God of mercy and grace,
>   we need no convincing of our guilt;
>   we need no persuading we are sinners;
>   the reality of our wrong is before us.

But we do need the prod to bring it all to voice.
We have convinced ourselves that if we remain silent,
>   you won't hear;
>   if we test our poisons underground, out of sight, in the dark,
>   no one will know, not even you.

So we nurse our grievous abuses, but they don't get well,
>   we carry our long-held grudges, and they just get heavier;
>   the ragged chips on our shoulders
>   become jagged blocks in our minds.

And broken covenant results in deceived broken body.

What will turn us?
What will make us attend to our ailing selves?
The promise of life, torment-free?
The possibility of days in joyful endeavor,
>   and nights of restful sleep?

Lord God, today we say it;
>   today we confess — we speak out our ugly word,
and receive your sweet forgiveness.

>   (A silence)

Now we have yielded our word to another;
O God, accompany us in transformed life,
now untouched by overwhelming distress,
now untroubled by life rendered weak by excessive demand
>   in the name of efficiency and success.

As we worship, and as we leave this place,
we exchange our word of ugliness
>   with glad cries of deliverance
>   and shouts of joy from a now upright heart.

In the name of the One of broken body,

AMEN.

PSALM 126

Like the psalmist, Lord God,
> we, too, have dreams,
> we, too, have hopes,
> we, too, look for restoration of good fortune.
So that we may laugh the laughter of pure joy
> and enjoy the song of fresh life from our lips.
Lord God, the depths of uncompromising winter,
> the fallow time of cold, unresponsive earth
has its counterpart in barrenness of soul
> and fruitlessness of endeavor.
But the fresh flower of spring and the maturing fruit of summer,
bring us to say,
"You have done great things for us!
All this plenty is not of our doing!
All is gifted to us!"
> and soul is lifted, and endeavor amply rewarded.
And while we are privileged to work with you,
> as we plough the field and scatter the good seed,
> or hoe garden and place potatoes, or parsley, or parsnip,
we can only stand and wait,
> wait for growth to happen,
> flowers to germinate,
> and finally, safely gather in the produce.
So Lord God, because you invite us to be part of the process,
> free us from believing we have absolute control over the process.
In spite of genetic engineering and biological control and measured fertilizer,
free us to praise, and wonder, and enjoy your good gifts.
And while we live our life of tears
> in bearing responsibilities too great for us,
> in carrying burdens too heavy for us,
intervene in our lives with a new word
> a word of burdens relinquished, of responsibilities shared
> a word of one once immersed in our world,
> now won in victory over a wintered world
> a word of resurrection.
Meantime, we wait for gift, surprising gift.

In the name of the One we are following,

AMEN.

PSALM 118:1–2, 19–29

Lord God,
>> we make claim to belong to you,
>> you, who are shown to be righteous.
> On that basis alone we linger at the gate,
>> so as to enter.

We enter hesitantly;
>> we are unsure of the battles already fought,
>> or the battles to come,
>> and how we may be asked to enter the battle.
> We enter unknowingly;
>> we have little to make us confident
>> except who you are — the cornerstone of all life;
>> but that is enough.
> We enter blindly
>> with enough faith for the day
>> and enough confidence to rejoice today;
>> but what of tomorrow?

We enter joyously,
>> with all the other entrants
>> feeding off the festive moment, in grand procession;
>> but will this last?
> We enter with betrayal, denial, abandonment and rejection
>> not far from our lives;
>> but for the moment, we keep them at bay,
>> with songs of blessing, affirmation, solidarity, and rejoicing.
> Still we enter, righteous, answering God
>> wondering at your stickability in offering steadfast love forever,
>> and wondering at our
>>> stickability to stay with you through the week.

But for the moment, hear our word of praise at the gate of the week.

In the name of the Righteous One,

AMEN.

PSALM 31:9–16

Lord God,
     abandoned one,
     forgotten, forsaken, forsworn;
     we stand with you awhile,
     awake a little.

Tears fall from eyes blood-red and wasted,
     sighing sorrow,
     dying morrow looms devilishly, but it's all opaque.

You are darkness, unseen, unloved, un-neighbored
     but we hold a heavy-on-wine tenuous grip of you, half asleep.
We've nearly forgotten your healing,
     your appealing word to outcast, leper, prostitute,
     forgotten enough to ban them from our assembly.

Why did you come into our lives?
We can't remember.
Even the whisperings about you have died.
Now we hear only the violent irrelevant curse of your name.

But they still come to get you
     if you raise your bloodied head in just protest.
"Irrelevance" is the cry of a rampant military
     backed by political religion gone narrow.

It is no surprise,
     and we nearly sleep;
     we can stand it no longer.

Will you lay us down slumber-dead
     while plotters scheme and schemers plot?

Tired trust waits for miracle
But meanwhile you are alone, God.

AMEN. We tried.

PSALM 22

Broken by a frightful Friday, Lord God,
    dehumanized to worm-like proportions;
    despised, depreciated, disparaged,
    but not ignored by foul mouths.

The only one who ignores the Son on this Friday
    is the One valued most,
    the One who brought him to birth,
    the One who suckled and nurtured him.

What has changed? What makes this Friday different?
Why have the wild bulls charged today?
Why do dogs circle to lunge at this wasted body on this Friday?
Why does the savagery of lions flaunt this Friday?

A chosen sacrifice for a chosen Friday;
    a convergence of history,
    a focus of God time and our time;
Jew and Gentile center on this fearsome Friday
    of dying and living,
    living and dying.

For our salvation,
    we have no choice but to live this Friday out to its death,
    forsaking God.

For you may yet turn.

And if you don't? — God help us.

AMEN.

PSALM 118:1–2,14–24

Today, Lord God, you call us to response,
    joyful response.
You open the way for our voice of praise,
    responding to your decisive and amazing intervention.
The conversation of Friday, which petered out to a mute finish,
    suddenly bursts into newness thought impossible.

And it is your doing;
    it is marvelous in our eyes.

We can talk again;
    we can shout and sing because the future —
    sealed behind a rolled up stone,
    guarded by men intent on diminishing truth out of existence,
    — the future breaks out today.

There is more to say on the day you made;
    the conversation keeps on;
we are not left to a lone anti-communion,
    masquerading as self-determination.

Our covenantal companion lives
    risen for righteous engagement
    engaged for righteous discourse,
    disgorged from earth for righteous partnership.

The gate opens,
    and it is your doing;
    it is marvelous in our eyes.

Praise to you, Lord God,
    heartfelt thanks —
    we have been found by ever-enduring steadfast love.

AMEN.

PSALM 150

Lord, our God,
      here in public worship we praise you,
      here from every corner of the sanctuary
         we join the voice of praise.

If the table of sacrifice and banquet were to praise,
      what would it say?
         Thanks be to God for the hundreds gathered here
            to covenant once more.
         Thanks for the hands breaking bread
            and pouring out life.
         Thanks for the feet that circle in ongoing promise.

If the baptismal font were to praise,
      what would it say?
         Thanks for little ones offered in trust.
         Thanks for vow confidently made.
         Thanks for entry into the people of God.

If the pews could speak in praise,
      what would they say?
         Thanks for the warmth of constant attendance.
         Thanks for active bodies bowed in prayer and singing
            for joy.
         Thanks for attentive listening for transforming word.

We praise you, God, from the sanctuary.

We pull out all stops, for your deserved doxology
      wind and strings resonate
      percussion and dance reverberate
      cymbal upon cymbal resound
      as breath echoes the voice of angels
         on this day of resurrection.

Praise the Lord!

AMEN.

PSALM 30

Lord, our God,
>we make our plea, for your sake and for ours;
>we draw your attention to our precarious circumstance;
>we claim your watchfulness,
>>for you and we are in crisis.

If we should perish,
>who will sing your praise?
>who will tell you can save?
>who will witness to the alternative story of good news?

Here is our crisis:
>— we are a product of our own inner life,
>— we nurse our grievances,
>— we nurture our hatreds,
>— we nullify forgiveness by unforgiveness,
>— we sabotage love by unwillingness to love.

We deny resurrection life by demanding retributive crucifixion,
>still reiterating Good Friday.

That is our crisis.
And, Lord God, it is your crisis.
Hear us! Be gracious to us!
Draw us up; heal us; lift up our lives; restore us to life.

Thrust us into resurrection life with your chosen one.
Dance with us the joyful dance of Easter life;
>so that our voice is let loose,
>and your penetrating word
>>does its healing work among the peoples.

Hear our prayer, we implore;
>in the name of the One gone before,

AMEN.

PSALM 23

God of the living,
O that we could sit with the psalmist in the quiet confidence
    that comes of many trust-filled conversations.

You are at the beginning and at the end,
    the bookends of unfolding stories,
        holding us upright.

We celebrate the quiet, refreshing moments of still satisfaction,
    savoring the restoration of our souls,
    and the energy for new direction.

We celebrate a presence, a mighty "Thou," beyond our understanding,
    in the dark places beset by evil, terror, and anxiety.

We celebrate communal times of bread and wine,
    in the warm glow of your sure love,
    where no biting enemy can snatch us.

Surely in the psalmist's seat there is satisfying atonement;
    clothed in goodness and mercy we are,
    sharing a dwelling place with the Lord of glory.

AMEN.

PSALM 148

You leave no part of your creation out, Lord God.
Every living thing is summoned to praise;
> the whole of creation is charged with worship;
> no gender or age is barred from a bidding to adoration.

The command is given;
The call is heard;
The warrant is discharged;
We, today, answer.

We answer with song and prayer, word of thanksgiving;
We answer with bowed posture;
We reorient our scattered selves around you, our creator
> banishing every other rival,
> displacing every other god,
> and placing you, Lord God, at the center
> > of our consciousness, our hopes, our plans.

Not all will respond,
> but we respond,
> gladly subpoenaed to appear before you.

May we represent our families?
May we deputize for our community?
May we stand in for our nation?
May we voice creation's praise to you?

And may you look kindly on your creation,
> allowing it to live one more day,
> permitting it another day to hope,
> granting it air and spirit to breathe,
> time for turning in repentant mood.

In the name of the Giver of resurrection days,

AMEN.

PSALM 67

Is it too much to assume, Lord, our God,
    that the earth's nations will find blessing
        through your people's praise?

Your promise to Abraham was such;
    through him all families of the earth would be blessed;
an awesome privilege,
an astonishing responsibility.

Your face to shine,
    that we might shine;
your blessing abundantly spread,
    that we might spread blessing;
your graciousness generously lavished,
    that we might be carriers of generous grace.

God, convict us if we are hoarders of blessing and grace,
    carefully walling in your life behind religious doors,
    enjoying ourselves in a fit of narcissism,
    harshly judging outsiders because of our insecurity inside.

God, spring us out as ambassadors,
    lever us beyond our religious comfort,
    into a world still hopelessly seeking for guidance.

Then the nations may have cause for gladness,
    and the peoples may discover a satisfying equity,
    and praise will be on the lips of every creature.

In the name of the One whose face shone in your presence,

AMEN.

PSALM 97

We come again this Sabbath, sedate in habit to routine ritual.
We come, with cursory greeting, to repose in customary pew,
    and lazy eye scans the ordered assembly,
        the Order of Service,
        the ordained entry.
And you come again, Lord God, this Sabbath.

You come in triumphant procession,
    hidden in holy darkness,
    with lightning accompaniment,
    supported by a rigorous righteousness and justice —
And we didn't see you.

Our minds were focused on lesser things;
    pale gods shadowed our vision,
    barren spirits proffered empty hopes,
    foul evilness diverted our intentions.
And we didn't see you.

We pause, to bow down,
    and in a dulled mind's eye search for a dawning.
We imagine you at your best —
    lover of good, and hater of evil, one who guards the faithful
    and gives them the justice denied them by the powerful.
But even our imaginings are half blind, and we only almost see you.

God, resurrect this hour;
    bring us back from the dead,
    to witness the procession of glory
    and so proclaim with the whole heavens,
    "The Lord is Sovereign over all the earth."
Then we will see you,
    and rejoice,
    and give thanks.
For you are wholly present, holy God.

AMEN.

PSALM 104:24–34, 35b

Lord God,
> in quiet, strong confidence you face your world,
> and we in company with praise-makers
>> look to you.

Our neighbors sing with us;
> all creatures sing with us,
>> living things, great and small,
>> mites to monsters,
> all rendered tame, robbed of fearfulness.

Differences are immaterial and no longer threaten
> because focus is on you, the giver.
Distinctions are tranquilized and no longer alarm
> because our gaze is not hobbled by other receivers.
Diversity is pacified and no longer distresses
> because our attentive devotion links
>> with your unbridled generosity.

If you are not fearful of the world's variety,
> then why should we fear?
If you are generous with all the creation,
> then why can't we live generously?
If you rejoice among all you made,
> then why can't we rejoice?

What freedoms you breathe on us this day,
> Lord, our God;
> freedoms encouraging embrace as large as yours;
> freedoms commanding respect as comprehensive as yours;
> freedoms provoking rejoicing as sweetly exuberant as yours.

Praise to you, Lord God,
> in the name of One breathing on us this day,

AMEN.

PSALM 8

Sovereign God,
of all the names we deal with daily,
> yours is the name we must finally deal with.
And of all the creatures you deal with daily,
> we are the creature you deal with most decisively.
> > Youngest or oldest,
> > naive or wise,
> > friend or foe,
> you are immersed in there, shaping, countering, crowning;
> dealing with us in heavenly ways,
> so we may deal humanely with the earth.
You, Sovereign God,
> you partner us, honor-crowned human beings
> > in the rule over creation.
But because we are near life's apex,
> we are seduced into thinking
> we are alone at life's apex,
> accompanying our perception with self-praise.
Stall us on that, Sovereign God,
> and carry us determinedly into creaturehood
> > in praise of its creator.
And because we are near life's apex,
> we are seduced into thinking
> > our responsibilities are toward you alone,
> > accompanying our perception with polished piety
> > and abdicated duty.
Stall us on that, Sovereign God,
> and lift us purposefully into authoritative vocation
> > as earth's stewards.

Sovereign God,
> deal with us daily
> and shape us as honor-crowned stewards.
Sovereign God,
> hear our daily praise,
> freeing us from creation's entrapment.

In the name of One who walked the line of praise and stewardship,

AMEN.

PSALM 96

Lord, our God,
>we say afresh today, "You rule the world!"

In our peculiar liturgy,
in this peculiar hour,
>we recognize no other authority.

Every other allegiance is beggared in this odd hour;
every other power is questioned in these curious rituals;
every other ordinance is subservient
>to the vow-taking of this unparalleled rite.

For none has ultimate power in our days or destiny.

We need tolerate no longer petty, oppressive powers;
we need endure no more inflicted injury;
we need give no licence to justice violated.
For none has ultimate power in our days or destiny.

Only you, Sovereign God, only you,
>celebrated in this peculiar hour.

So we sing, sing, sing;
so we bless, tell, declare,
>in the company of these families,
>and to all who twist truth and subvert justice,
>"The Lord is King" — there is no other;
>and we follow this sovereign into a new order,
>>a new government, a new premiership,
>recognized even by heaven and earth
>>sky and sea
>>field and forest.

Sovereignty belongs to you, Lord God,
>creator, judge, and actor in our midst.

In the name of the One who lived among us,

AMEN.

PSALM 146

Lord, our God,
>in a world out of control,
>we discover we do have control.

We can direct our souls toward praise;
>we can form the words of "Hallelujah"
>and sing them in high praise.
We place your name and your praise
>in the same phrase
>and direct our adulation toward you,
>>our living Lord.

And it makes a difference, thank God;
>for we may now discern where to invest trust,
>with whom to credit integrity,
>on what criteria we judge faithfulness;
it is the One who deserves our unreserved praise.

Whom we choose to praise makes a difference, thank God;
>for we may now recognize injustice
>>when we mingle with you who executes justice;
>we may now appreciate prisoner circumstance
>>when we relate to you who frees captive people;
>we may now discover the blind ones,
>>the bowed down, the stranger,
>>because we see through your eyes
>>to the broken ones in our midst.

Our praise makes a difference, thank God,
>for we now mark wickedness before it devours us,
>we now discriminate against perishing pathways,
>we now withhold trust from the untrustworthy.
Thank you, Lord God, for the gift of unusual perception,
>and give us the gumption to direct our souls praise-ward,
>in honor of you, our maker.

In the name of One who made a difference,

AMEN.

PSALM 5:1–8

Lord God,
>without embarrassment we address you whom we cannot see,
>you whom we neither touch nor hear,
>yet you, more real than me and every other one gathered today.

For we have appealed to our neighbors,
>and discover they have feet of clay as we have;

we have appealed to ourselves,
>desperately seeking firm groundedness within
>>but discover shifting sands and poverty of resources;

we have appealed to impartial counselors,
>but discover the same vested interests and prejudices
>>and lack of innocence that we have.

Neighbors, self, and stranger share our distorted realities.
We have run out of options,
>so with boldness and diffidence,
>with desperation and determination,

we appeal to you.
In public worship, in your house,
>on your holy patch, using your Word,

we request a hearing.
For our world has gone wrong
>in the hands of deceitful practitioners of lies:

— our realities are perverted
>by the dim-sighted vision of the boastful self-aggrandized powerful,

— our hearing is distorted
>by those who delight in their own wickedness.

Who will listen to us, but you?
Who is the "who" that will counter the crookedness
>of pretenders to center?

You, Lord God, you, only you,
>can fill the vacuum left
>when every other claimant is proven inadequate.

We thus speak with you,
>the only one who has real claim to partner our conversation.

And we do that here, today, in public worship,
>and we watch and wait with patient urgency.

In the name of One who spoke with you frequently,

AMEN.

PSALMS 42 and 43

Lord God,
 it is not as easy as that, and you know it.
Downcast souls, disquieted souls,
 don't easily slide to hopeful praise.
That way for us is jagged, crater-obstacled, obstructed
 by former depressions, rupturing hurts still active,
 inferior choices made when we knew everything.
But our longing is strong,
 our yearning bursts beyond our hoping,
 our thirsting for satisfying communion
  searches for quenching contentedness.
Do you know our plight, Lord God?
People in public places taunt us:
 they say that you, God, don't care,
 and shamefacedly we grimly endure,
  with private tears and defected hearts.
We make stands for justice,
 but you fail to back us
  and we look foolish, forlorn, forgotten,
 so we settle for meager acts of kindness.
We have great memories of your once history;
 you promised and gave a place for homecoming;
 you permitted a home for worship
  and issues of shares in holiness;
 you granted neighbors of joy,
 thronging festival processions that lifted our souls
  to glad contentedness.
Yes, we remember.
What has happened, O God?
When will you respond to these anguished souls?
When will you overwhelm our well-disciplined apathy?
When will you restore, go beyond our former communion of glad joy?
We wait in hope,
 and we will again praise you,
for odds are that
 our peculiar mix of anguish and doxology
 may turn you to our needful souls.
Hear our prayer, O Lord, for the sake of your honor.

AMEN.

PSALM 77:1–2, 11–20

Lord God,
>   you have a reputation for intervening when lost ones cry out;
the reports record your radical reordering of power
>   in favor of abused ones;
the witnesses consistently attest to your intruding into people's affairs
>   and acting on behalf of the defenseless.

All that is lodged in our memory from early days,
>   fuel for meditation
>   fodder for imagination
>   grist for remembering, remaking of life.
For we surely need it to reorder our own out-of-sync rhythms.

Live with us, O God, as we recite the saving events.
Breathe with us through your people's portrayal of their life-receiving.
Spill your holiness onto us,
>   as we recount your life of holiness among us.

For you turned barrenness into life giving;
>   you saved our conniving, proud ancestors
>   from their own cunning pride;
>   you rescued families from powerfully sure entrapment;
>   you opened up a third way
>   between certain dying and certain drowning;
>   you led in our dark times with your light
>   and governed in ungovernable wilderness;
>   you gifted us guidelines and administering priests
>   in our time of disarray;
we followed as safely as sheep follow their shepherd.

Lord God,
>   you still are in the business of overthrowing the overwhelming
>   and underwriting the undervalued.

Surround us, then, with your holy presence
>   and order our out-of-sync rhythms of life
>   within us and between us.

In the name of the Holy One always in tune,

AMEN.

PSALM 30

Lord God,
there was once a time when we were so sure;
    sure of who you were,
    sure of how you should act,
    sure of how we should act,
    sure of how others ought to act.
We appealed to absolutes and ran out of freshness;
    we knew too much and heard no new word;
    we overstepped boundaries and violated others' freedoms.
We thought we were prosperous,
    over-endowed with favor;
    "never will it happen to me" was our quick confidence.
But it did happen, and we can name the occasion;
    favor hid itself,
    grace abandoned us,
    dismay came to stay,
    crucifixion shrouded our bright days.
And some of us, Lord God, cry out of crucified lives;
    lonely abandonment demolished our confidence
    and we cry to you for new life,
    unable to cry to you in praise.
And some of us, Lord God, are raised as wiser ones,
    profoundly glad you are biased to help,
    tilting toward us and not against us,
    prone to healing,
    leaning to restoration.
For your saving prejudice toward seekers
    causes us to praise you;
    abandoning sterile absolutes in favor of living relationship,
    relinquishing pitiful glumness in favor of morning joy,
    quitting smug knowingness
        in favor of witnessing to our own truth,
    with thankfulness for new life,
    committed to new perceptions of your loving self.
This is your way with us, and our way with you, Lord God.

AMEN.

PSALM 82

Lord God,
>   you mark yourself off from the other gods,
>   and you occupy places we hesitate to inhabit.
For you don't line your pockets with percentage take,
>   you don't concern yourself with self-serving,
>   you don't retreat to the sumptuous silence of heaven,
>   untouched by the plight of the poor.
To our chagrin
>   you won't authorize acquisitiveness,
>   you won't applaud consumerism,
>   you won't endorse the division of "haves" and "have nots."
You embarrass us, Lord God,
>   with your constant talk of the lowly destitute,
>   your steadfast partiality to the needy weak,
>   your undeviating fondness for the displaced orphan.
And then you ask us to follow you?
O God, we are torn between allegiance to you
>   and nodding to the gods we love to control.
We haven't the nerve to follow a God
>   who breaks ranks with the other gods,
>   and enters the messiness of the world,
>   a messiness we so desperately seek to escape.
Our courage fails us when we see you move so purposefully
>   toward conversation with fringe folk, folk we prefer to avoid.
So, Lord, our God,
>   when you rise up to make your judgments,
>   when you repeat all these claims in the presence of the gods,
>   remember our frailty,
>   our shaky resolve,
>   our fearful duplicity;
but remember we are learners, learning still,
>   faith-bearers learning faithfulness,
>   sinners learning to stand as covenantal partners with you.
And take us today as far as we can go in obedience,
>   without guilt paralysis,
>   with the courage we have.

In the name of the obedient courageous One,

AMEN.

PSALM 52

Those like green olive trees,
    with roots in liturgy and word, are rare, Lord God.
Those with lively trusting faith,
    who feed on worship resources, are unusual.

For we, God, are more familiar with mischief-makers,
    schemers, sharp operators;
we know about law-makers with dubious ethics
    and law-keepers with questionable morals.
We are aware of those whose intention is evil
    and are ready to sacrifice goodness for personal gain.
We are dismayed when lying is more normal than truth telling,
    and brutal, malignant language is more prevalent
        than sympathetic, charitable speech.

But, Lord God, we know these things
    because they are in us,
    they shadow us,
    they are our second nature.
So we are more dismayed when we know
    our own capacity for treachery.

God, may we collaborate with you in breaking down our evil
    and tearing out our destructive plotting,
and uprooting our deceitful intent,
and may we laugh at such behavior
    with the derisive laughter it deserves.
So today we come,
    fledgling olive trees, peace-finders
        peace-makers
        peace-keepers
heralds of new life, rooted in worship,
    proclaiming your name,
    weighted away from lies and riches,
    weighted toward your steadfast love.

In the name of the One we follow,

AMEN.

PSALM 85

Lord God, we wait to hear what you will speak.
We have heard before your conversation with your people.
We heard stories of your restoring Jacob, and Jacob's people;
     saved from famine, given good land;
     saved from an oppressive empire, given freedom;
     saved from precarious wilderness life, given promised land.
All through, you gave and forgave.
And we heard stories of sibling rivalry,
     of parental favoritism, of surrogate motherhood.
We heard stories of divorced kings,
     murderous prophets, crooked priests.
Drugs, betrayal, rape, murder, political intrigue,
     a state too greedy for tax
     all figure in the stories of your people.
You, Lord God, were never shocked or surprised;
you were angered and anguished
     as your covenantal partner in conversation
        wrecked the relationship.
So, Lord God, any story you may find among us today
     will not shock or surprise you,
     but will you be angered and anguished
     as you view your current covenantal partner in conversation?
Lord God, for our part in this hour
     we are honest about our stories
     as you are honest about the stories that pass before your Word;
we present you with an uncensored version this day,
     as you present an uncensored Word to us this day.
And for our part we plead for mercy and restoration,
     revival and salvation.
So that at least in this hour
     steadfast love and faithfulness will meet
     and righteousness and peace will court and kiss
     and faithfulness and righteousness may envelop the world.
All to your glory, our God, and to our peaceful well-being.

In the name of One who spoke honestly with us,

AMEN.

PSALM 107:1–9, 43

Lord God,
      it takes little imagination to picture today's refugees
            wandering in trackless places,
            finding no home,
for homelessness is common in our world,
      a world of hungry, thirsty, fainting ones.

The homeless ones there
      cry out of trouble,
a trouble we may even harbor here
      in our community, families, selves.

Hear the cry, our God,
      whether it is here at hand, or there far away.

As we are delivered from distress here,
      may they be delivered from distress there.

As we are being led home here,
      may they be led home there.

As we are satisfied with good food and clean water here,
      may they be satisfied with good food and clean water there.
And may they and we give thanks
      for your steady love for all humanity.

God, gatherer of lost ones,
      whose gathering hand reaches over all compass points,
      gather all your people home, we pray,
      into forgiven community.

And who is it that brings us to God's many-roomed home?

Only Jesus Christ.
I tell you in his name we are forgiven.

THANKS BE TO GOD!

PSALM 50:1–8, 22–23

Lord God, today you speak.
Today you do not invite conversation,
    and we are not used to that.
We would prefer reasonable negotiation;
    we expect some give and take;
    we anticipate a degree of compromise;
after all, are you not like us?
No, not today! Today you speak.
You speak abruptly, not ushered in to worship by our song of praise.
You summon us with undue haste, not waiting for our usual bidding.
You require that we hear, not waiting for our meager payment.
Surely you need our praise, our bidding, our offering
    as a cue for your entry.
No, not today! Today you speak.
You emerge out of silence
    with searing tempest and thunderous conviction,
    demanding our attention, we who say we follow you.
We will listen, Lord God.
We will control our fit of juvenile pique,
    and practice the obedient stance of a follower,
    for we might indeed learn something.
Speak to us today.
Lay before us the demands of your covenant.
Link us in to God-honoring and neighbor-care.
Gather us in to acquiescence to your sovereignty,
    and respect for humanity.
Hold us in to your holiness, and reverence for friend and stranger.
For if you don't, we will continue to dishonor you,
    and threaten our neighbor, and violate our own well-being.
Speak with us today
    as we humbly bring our meager selves
        in thanksgiving offering.
Perhaps we may discover afresh, you who sets our way.

In the name of One who showed the way,

AMEN.

PSALM 80:1–2, 8–19

Lord, our God,
> you once led your people.
You led them with clear vision,
> and firm resolve,
> and a bold purposefulness
>> that amazes us.
Today at worship we see the signs of your former self:
Music that touches heaven's gates
> that we did not compose.
Lyrics that offer a rhetoric of beauty and nerve
> we did not form.
Architecture that imposes awe and communion
> we did not dream of.
All spawned from our forebears, who lived in your light
> and lived out their faithful obedience.
All signs of your sure life-giving and their courageous responding.
So your Word went out to every nation,
> every city and hamlet, every town and village,
> world over,
> until it came to our town, our congregation.
But now it has paused, still bearing the old signs,
> but hesitating to live the ancient courage,
>> the former faith, the costly communion.
Turn again, O God of Hosts.
Attend to the Word, which is vandalized by neglect,
> and hogged by the religious,
> and perishing from muted personal ownership.
Turn again, O Lord God of Hosts,
> and restore what you once planted in our midst.
Strengthen us as fit carriers of good news,
> bold bearers of salvation stories,
> tamers of timidity,
> lovers of justice,
> advocates for neighbor care;
all to your glory and the life of your word to humanity.

AMEN.

PSALM 71:1–6

Lord God,
>   unless you take a lead with us,
>   our lives will always be the same;
our view of self and world will never change;
and some of us want that.
But some of us are in brokenness;
we wear bruises,
carry heavy hurt,
shamed by events beyond our ability to influence,
or shamed by events we influenced too much.
We seek a refuge, a safe place to tell the truth of our lives,
truth which, when heard,
>   will meet graciousness and not scorn,
>   meet trustful, kindly gentleness and not contempt.
Lord God,
rescue us to be truth tellers and truth hearers;
for unless you take a lead with us,
our lives will always be the same;
>   bruised, heavy hurted, shamed.
And rescue us from gossipy truth-pryers,
or truth-pryers who possess instant answers,
or truth-pryers too keenly aware of appropriate correction;
for unless you take a lead with them,
their lives will always be the same.
For it is you, Lord, who are our hope,
and it is in you we trust —
trust learnt from our years of trading in truth with you.
So our praise is in our hearts,
on our lips,
in our community,
because we tell truth to one who carefully listens,
taking a lead with us,
so our lives will not be the same.

In the name of the One who is the truth,

AMEN.

PSALM 81:1, 10–16

Lord God,
>   you spoke to our forebears
>   and they spoke to us.
We hear their witness over the ages
>   of your word in law and story,
>   commandment and history,
>   Torah and narrative.
It couldn't be plainer.
But would they listen to the stories they repeated?
And would we listen to their testimony?
It seems both they and we switched channels
>   and listened to other voices.
We severed promising lines with you and preserved
>   easier lines, suspect lines, seductive lines.
We have slid under the spell of our own inadequate wisdom,
>   always claiming proud rightness,
>   always surrounded by deathly wrongness.
The equation doesn't balance,
>   and our last defense is
>   "If they would only listen to me...."
Lord God, squash that arrogance
>   and gift us with listening ear tuned to your voice.
For we are appalled at last week's abuse,
>   yesterday's murder, the current corporate rip-off,
>   the present crisis, today's war;
and we crave for resolution,
>   satisfied bellies, safety from the abusing powerful,
for our babies,
>   our adolescents, our midlifers,
>   our elderly, our disregarded
>   in every community.
But Lord God,
>   you have granted us one more hearing,
>   so it depends today on our listening.
We are here.
In the name of One who brings your word,

AMEN.

PSALM 139:1–6, 13–18

Lord God,
> every one of us present this day has fragile beginnings;
> every one of us is wonder born, frail, but protected;
gifted with body and life, softly nourished,
safely fingered into form,
known, seen, scanned, before human eye beheld.

What gentle persistence you have with us, O Lord.
What touching attentiveness you maintain
> from our first fragile moments.
What delicate gift you give
> in the first paragraphs of our personal story.
Before any word was on our lips,
> your words about each one were booked;
> you reserved our place in your world.

How we have scuttled the original plot.
How we have tampered with the unfolding,
> deforming life into tearing tangle.
For we have attempted our own script,
> fearing our transitoriness,
> and seeking a permanence of power not ours to take.

Forgive us, O God, and give us the attention once given;
> for our early fragility still holds;
> yet perchance we are supple enough for your new direction
> before our souls break in brittleness;
> for we never escape your searching,
> your knowingness,
> your acquaintance with our waywardness.

Look kindly on us, O Lord,
> as you did in our first passionate linking and dividing moments.
Caress us with kindness, once given — again;
> kiss us with love, once given — again;
and we will wait with wonder,
> born again into your new world of promise.

In the name of One born among us,

AMEN.

PSALM 14

Lord God, today in this place we publicly announce
    your name in our hearing.
We do not wish to be counted among the foolish
    who practice a secret atheism.
We would shun kinship with those
    who fail to acknowledge a sovereign life outside their own lives.
We will not be drawn into the circle of those
    whose lives are closed to the Deity.
For we have seen lives wrecked, unhinged,
    shallow, and empty of purpose
    because no room is given for your presence.
We have seen lives aggressive, destructive, abusive, exploitative
    because of no ethic except what is self-serving.
We have seen lives corrupt, greedy, devious, dishonorable
    because of no reference to power
    beyond the personally engendered.
And we recognize these things
    because they are resident within, capable of expression,
    lodged in the secret heart, out of view from public scrutiny.
So we pause in public worship
    and ask, "What part of my heart practices this awful atheism?"
As you look from heaven, what do you see, Lord God?
We would not be too proud, O God.
We make no claim to innocence.
We admit to more than a dollop of foolishness in us.
We own up to our perversive straying
    and beg for your mercy.
So in this hour
    we entertain a new thought,
    a thought born of wisdom,
    that within and without, with heart and with voice,
    we acknowledge you as our Lord
    and see ourselves among your righteous,
        touching rejoicing, tasting gladness
    as people saved from clutches of terror.

Hear our prayer in the name of One who saved,

AMEN.

PSALM 79:1–9

Lord God, can you hear us?
Will you hear us this day?
For we have words to say that are not often spoken
    and feelings to vent seldom admitted;
all the more difficult because we are trained in the nuances
    of Sabbath civility and pulpit politeness.
Our Sunday dress covers our inner indignation;
our ordered worship denies our disordering inner turmoil.
We dare not utter words of wrath and resentment,
    for what will you think of us?
    what will our neighbor think?
    what will we think of ourselves?
So we have nicely buried our seething fury,
    and we present for public display
    our pristine piety in the hope you will like us.
But, Lord God, it is no good,
    for a real part of our mental innards is suppressed,
    and it takes its toll on our bodies.
So hear our truth, you who traffic in truth;
    for we are crucified daily;
    we light-carriers always get burnt;
    we with sacred sense helplessly watch holy things violated,
    and it riles.
Bitter resentment heart-swells within,
    as sneering secularists grab to destroy spiritual life
    and depreciate hallowed values.
We burst in rage, in passionate ire at such unappreciative provocation.
Why do they do it?
Why stomp on all that is lovely, and pure, and peace-making?
Why are the guardians of holy things disdainfully dismissed,
    despised, contemptuously cast aside?
God, we get angry; and we are not sorry.
Because your glory is ground down,
    and our valued hopes evaporate in the violence.
Interject into the malignant, turbulent conversation of our days,
    and pastor your flock again, for your name's sake.

AMEN.

PSALM 91:1–6, 14–16

God Most High, you know us too well;
      of all those we speak with
      you appreciate best of all our predicament.
For *here* in worship we are in touch with your sovereign greatness,
      your majestic transcendence;
and *there* in the week we are besieged by snaring fowlers
      and deadly pestilence
      and terror nights and arrow-piercing days.
Here, in worship's safe place, you raise the matter;
      you add a week's rending tension to the devotional agenda,
      encouraging us to acknowledge the real world.
For our world is dangerous,
      beset as we are by fatal disease
      or lethal abuse
      or disastrous brutalities.
And out of mischief, or ignorance,
      we expunge such talk from the liturgical conversation
          in nice denial.
But you call our attention to the sinister segment of our place in space,
      encouraging us to acknowledge the real world.
God Most High,
God of sovereign greatness and majestic transcendence,
      speak with us in this safe place;
      speak of life's dread with verbal pointers
          for a safe week's journey,
journeys tagged with not fearing,
          snatched from danger,
          honor rescued, covered refuge,
          companioned faithfulness,
      so that we may negotiate our passage through the week,
      and be delivered, protected,
      to call on you next week from this seat,
      knowing of you and known by you,
          our conversational partner:
God Most High
God of sovereign greatness
      and majestic transcendence.

AMEN.

PSALM 137

Lord God, in our worship we sing our glad songs of praise,
    songs loaded with promising hope and buoyant trust,
        weighted with confident assurance;
    songs coming from optimistic faith,
    solid, satisfying songs, joyful songs, inspiring songs.
Songs easy to sing
    for those of us who have never grieved over loss,
    and those of us who have never suffered brutality,
    and those of us who have never hoped for much.
We will never be disappointed
    and our song will sweet-syrup our spiritual diet
        in palatable portions, enough for one day.
But for those of us enduring savage loss,
those of us distraught by time's fiendish scarring
    and today's raw wounding,
those of us whose peaceful homecoming is ripped from our grasp,
    and our only resource is intense, fervent hope,
we weep our way through the songs,
    forced by convention and conformity to follow the melody,
    but nowhere croaking our line of discord
        that jars our inner harmonies.
Lord God, we hate the men who wound us
    we loath those systems people that strip humanity naked
    we detest the social forces legitimated by vote
        and manipulating design, which kidnap our integrity.
We lay these repugnant estrangements before you, Lord God,
    with all the acrimony we can muster,
    and we leave them to your wisdom.
Meanwhile, we worship.
We contemplate forgiving as part of our healing.
We seek a fresh homecoming for stable recovery.
We anticipate whole restoration where
    we may sing in unrestrained joy within your sacred home.
And our hope flows in healthy sparkle,
    for you, Lord God, have heard our wounded voice this day.

In the name of the wounded One, honest before you,

AMEN.

PSALM 66:1–12

Lord, our God,
> we come freely, unfettered,
> generously permitted to enter this space of worship.
We come in public worship,
> obeying the call to praise.
We come with our stories,
> stories of snared cornering and amazing release,
> stories of heavy burdening and surprising lightening,
> stories of sore testing and astonishing endurance.
All our stories, and every part of our stories,
> fall within your powerful concern.
Nothing happens outside your jurisdiction.
Your authority pervades all the affairs of the nations
> and secretes its way in to our own stories.
So we stand with confidence here;
> we are not at the mercy of random events;
> we are in the stream of your liberating desires;
> we walk on prepared paths
>> through overwhelming odds stacked against us.
And we joyously survive.
With story in hand, confident of your overseeing,
> salvation enjoyed, and worship space to do it,
> we indulge for the hour in praise, doxology,
>> song of thanksgiving,
> and bursting pride in your gifting us
>> the observation powers to acknowledge
>> your great deeds in the earth.
Who else does that?
Who else notices, then gives praise?
Who else links earth's events and our adventures with you,
> Sovereign God?
We do, and we are glad, companion God,
> for we are not alone, but in sovereign company.

Thanks be to God.

AMEN.

PSALM 119:97–104

Lord God,
> you provide the ultimate incentive for good living;
> a pure sweetness in a world of bitterness,
> a tasting for good life beyond compare.

For six days we are force-fed on a diet of demand and seduction,
> crammed, stuffed with words
>> which blare, slide, pamper, assault;
> words which entice, persuade, attack, deceive.

For six days we are word-weary, bloated, blasted, brutalized, gorged
> with no more stomach for the world's indigestible provision.

Not on this seventh day!

Oh for the taste of your refreshing word,
> your food for thought
>> giving access to your fellowship table.

For we savor your guiding commands,
> which feed our souls and muscle our intellect;

we feast on your promises,
> which give us stamina for a week long;

we sip on your decrees and precepts,
> which give us maturity beyond our years
> and save us from easy exhaustion
>> in a morally deficient world.

For in this value-provisioned home of worship
> we discover the fare for wholesome living,
> and we learn to discriminate
>> nurture sustenance from junk fodder.

So, Lord, our God, chef supreme, connoisseur of delight,
> revive our appetite for cherishable faith;
> give us resolve for body-building this community of faith;
> grant us the sweet aftertaste of your ordinances to last the week
>> 'til we sit at faith table once more.

In the name of One who taught life at parties,

AMEN.

PSALM 65

Lord God, God of holy place and every place,
  we come into liturgy once more,
  to indulge in wonder-making perceptions of your creation again,
  our weekly reminder of your re-creation
  in our flattened, mechanical, fated perceptions of our world.
Lord God,
  we come into your new world,
  away from our commodity-ridden deceptions of value,
  away from our thoughtless consumer efficiencies,
  away from our sense of powerful control,
    and into a liturgy of fascinating bewilderment,
    a form of awesome surprise,
    an order of amazing serendipity.
For who is it who establishes the mountain rock
  the grain of timber
  the velvet petal?   Not us.
And who is it who stills a raging storm
  calms a trouble
  brings the balmy days?   Not us.
And who is it who makes a colored dawn
  and brilliant dusk
  and aurora light?   Not us.
Your well-ordered earth produces its bounty
  season by season, valley by valley,
  field by field, plant by plant,
  grain by grain, overflowing wagons bringing overflowing cups.
So in our liturgy we concede to your intended ordered environment
  for our vow taking
  our forgiveness asking
  our enjoyment making
  our soul's satisfying
  our singing together for joy
    peculiar to people admitting
    your astonishing ascendancy
    in liturgy, world, and earth.

In the name of the conversing, answering One,

AMEN.

PSALM 119:137–144

Lord God,
> a sadness cloaks us and distressing zeal envelops us
> when men and women tramp on your truth,
>> trivializing it to insignificance,
>> filling religious air space with banal pastimes
>> devoting godly column inches to shallow fancies
>> killing holy time with trifling programs.

Lord God,
> who appreciates the fine nuances of your word?
> who values the delicate touch of your decrees?
> who gauges the rich depths of your precepts?

But even in our clumsy handling of your law,
> your clear truth touches our crude hoping;

even in our weekly cursory glance at chosen text,
> your penetrating righteousness oozes through
>> to our awkward justice-making;

even in our green, wet-behind-the-ears
>> grappling with your commandments,
> your sure promise dents our well-polished armored piety.

So our sadness is on two fronts:
> others don't appreciate the knowing finesse
>> of your language with us,
> and we might skim the surface too.

Lord God, our plea from our small corner
> is courage to stay silent enough
> to hear your well-tried promises,
> to take your promises and live them in righteous living,
> to delight in loving your word
>> and loving all word-hearers in this communion,
> and to gather understanding that nurtures us
>> beyond existing toward abundant living.

Lord God,
> is that too much to ask?

For we do ask it in the name of One who lived that way,

AMEN.

PSALM 145:1–5, 17–21

Sovereign Lord God, you guide with tender kindness,
 like our dearest friend and closest neighbor,
and yet you rule in glorious splendor,
 in a manner worthy of the greatest respect and highest esteem.
Your way of playing your covenantal role baffles us,
 as if there were no boundaries for you too difficult to cross,
 no task you would shirk, no mission you would refuse.
"Unsearchable greatness" is the word.
So we will praise you in this mystery
 and rest in your awesome neighborly presence
nervous and at ease; apprehensive and confident; amazed and secure.
For what God has vital interest in babies and in old people?
What God converses with adolescent and midlifer?
What God loves both friend and stranger?
What God accompanies the walkers on the faultline
 between ethnic groups, gender groups, age groups?
What God gives unfettered attention to the needy broken,
 the bowed-down falling?
You go beyond the bounds of what is reasonable,
 or practical, or politically sensible.
Do you really come near to *all* who call on you?
 or is it only some favorites who are blessed?
And who judges whether it is a true call?
Do you really pay attention to *all* who fear you?
 or is it only select God-fearers who receive your kindly attention?
And who judges the God-fearers' stance?
Do you really watch over *all* who love you?
 or is it only the overt lovers we see each week?
And who judges true love?
God, it baffles us; the way is wider than our narrow limiting.
But why waste time baffled? Why not rejoice?
We will; for our part, we will bless your holy name
 — resting in your astonishing self-giving,
 — praising you in your regal power,
 — thankful it is you who are our God and no other.

In the name of the One who embodied such Godliness,

AMEN.

PSALM 98

Lord God, please don't find us lagging in the liturgy.
With great effort we get ourselves here,
   and there is every reason why we might not have come.
Our thoughts trail behind our bodies,
   desperately making every effort to catch up.
And we engage this liturgy,
   formed in the exhaustion of last week,
   tired in its familiarity and constant wear.
Now speak with us, we pray,
   for self-engendered praise boomerangs;
   self-manufactured thanksgiving becomes diverted
     into giving thanks to self,
 — an enjoyable fabrication, a pleasant facade.
So speak with us, we pray.
We listen for your word, your summons to all creation
   to explode in wild joy;
calling roaring sea, boiling foam in sparkling fury unleashing its power,
   flooding the earth with powerful praise;
commanding hills unfolding, reaching high,
   rolling through shadow and light,
   gathering momentum to a climax of syncopated adulation;
requiring every pipe, every string, every percussion played in harmony,
   a song rising/falling crescendo combining in orchestral beauty
     in tribute of applause.
Lord God, if sea, hill, and string can flood the earth with peals of gladness,
   so can we.
For your reliable, ordered, celebrating creation
   forms the context of our hopeful liturgy.
But we know more.
Your righteousness,
your steadfast love,
your faithfulness,
shower us, beam on us, mantle us,
   and your victory over demonic bonding frees us
   to spring in praise we thought beyond our capacity.
So hear our song,
   sung in the name of One remembering us kingdom hopefuls,

AMEN.

PSALM 46

Lord, our God
    we have walked the path of this year
    we participated in the stream of the ages
        seeking, waiting, searching,
        looking for the dawning holy habitation of the Most High.
How many times have we recited,
    "Your Kingdom come on earth as it is in heaven"?
We watched nations vie for power—
    military, economic, diplomatic,
    territorial, ethnic, political;
and did they make it?
Some hold tenuous supremacy reinforced by threat and fear;
    and all brink on tottering,
    anxiously plastering up crumbling edges.
And while all that happens around us,
Sunday by Sunday we take our place in public worship,
    tasting the city that will not totter.
For here in worship we savor early, residency in your City:
    here we learn the citizenship necessary in the Holy City,
    here we discover that victory based on coercion
        is no victory at all;
    here we discover your ways, Lord God,
    repeat your lines,
    like, "Stop fighting and know that I am God!";
    here we are the apprentices learning Holy City building;
    here we are novices in training, imbibing Holy City ways;
    here we are eavesdroppers overhearing Holy City language.
The nations' instability threatens humanity's well-being,
    but we place our trust in you, Lord God of Hosts,
    as chief architect of the Holy City
    for which you graciously give foretaste and tuition.
Refuge-making God,
God, builder of majesty proportions,
God, founder of bow- and spear-free zones,
    we enjoy your home.

In the name of One who prepares a place for us,

AMEN.

Bibliography

Brueggemann, Walter. *The Message of the Psalms.* Minneapolis: Augsburg Press, 1984.

_____. *Abiding Astonishment: Psalms, Modernity, and the Making of History.* Literary Currents in Biblical Interpretation. Louisville: Westminster/John Knox Press, 1991.

_____. "Exodus," in *The New Interpreters Bible,* Vol 1. Nashville: Abingdon Press, 1994.

Fretheim, Terence E. *Exodus.* Interpretation. Louisville: John Knox Press, 1991.

Mays, James L. *Psalms.* Interpretation. Louisville: John Knox Press, 1994.

Savron, George W. *Telling and Retelling; Quotation in Biblical Narrative.* Bloomington, Indiana: Indiana University Press, 1988.

Weiser, Artur. *The Psalms: A Commentary.* Old Testament Library. Philadelphia: Westminster Press, 1965.

Index